THE NĀTHA PHILOSOPHY AND ASHṬĀṄGA-YOGA

THE NĀTHA PHILOSOPHY AND ASHṬĀṄGA-YOGA

DR. V.S. BHATNAGAR

ADITYA PRAKASHAN,
NEW DELHI

First published: 2012

ISBN 978-81-7742-120-0

₹600/.00

Published by Aditya Prakashan, 2/18, Ansari Road,
New Delhi – 110 002.
email: contact@adityaprakashan.com
website: www.adityaprakashan.com

Printed at D.K. Fine Arts Press (Pvt.) Ltd., Delhi – 110 052.

CONTENTS

PREFACE

These are brief studies in the philosophy of the Nātha Sampradāya, a socio-religious movement, if one may like to call it, which spread fast with its hundreds of *āsanas* or monasteries transcending borders and boundaries and cutting across regions and historical times from Afghanistan to Bengal and from Kedarnāth in the north to the deep down south, having a central body to serve as a regulating authority of some sort. The *sampradāya* which came to the fore about 1150 A.D. under Mahā Yogī Gorakshanātha, an author of several works on the philosophy of the sect, preached equality of all people irrespective of all distinctions, and that one can experience oneness with the highest Reality, the Supreme Soul, Para Brahman, who by His own will creates the Universe through His Śakti inseparable from Him, the whole cosmic world being unfoldment of the Divine Śakti in Her diverse forms, and that the supreme object of the *yoga mārga* advocated by him was to realise that the soul of every individual was non-different from the Universal Soul, and that it was realisable by self-experience under the guidance of a self-realised spiritual guide, without taking recourse to external formalities, rituals and dogmas, thus giving hope even to the weakest and the lowliest who can by intense awareness and mental observation of one's true nature and by deep meditation and reflection can realise the Supreme Reality.

Gorakshanātha's *yoga-mārga* was deeply rooted in the ancient *yogic* traditions of India, traceable to varying extent no doubt, to the *Vedas, Upanishads, Smṛitis, Yoga-Sūtra, Purāṇas* and other works. He never alluded anywhere that he was deviating from or protesting, much less revolting, against the spiritual and philosophical traditions of the land. He believed that by synthesising the views of different schools of philosophy and religions, and by following the *Yoga-mārga,* state of *viśrānti,* which marks the cessation of *chitta-vṛittis*, is achieved and the *yogī* is absorbed in Para-Brahman-Parmeśvara. And this is possible even when not living in seclusion but while striving for the welfare and happiness of the people. His description of an *Avadhūta* sets highest ideals for an individual, a morally and spiritually elevated person who has realised the true nature of Self.

In its original format, the work, "*Some Aspects of the History and Philosophy of the Nātha Sampradāya*", was divided into two parts. Part I deals with the problems related to the Ādi Siddhas, the Nava-Nāthas, the three Mahāyogīs, viz. Matsyendranātha, Gorakshaṇātha and Jālandharanātha, some of the important practices among the Nāthas, their distinctive marks, the complex problem of the Nātha sub-sects or *Panthas* and a longish chapter on the Nātha *āsanas* or monasteries in India, mainly in c.1820 A.D. and c.1924 A.D. showing spectacular spread of the sect. Part II, which is being published first for reasons explained below, deals with the Nātha philosophy, and forms the more important part of the work.

It was felt that though Part I was complete in most respects, it still suffered from a draw-back viz., the information and data about the present actual position of the sect, its sub-sects, the condition of the Nātha monasteries and the role they are playing in the changed circumstances was as yet incomplete, and its completion was likely to take at least a year more. We have the required information and figures for c.1820 A.D. and also for c.1924 A.D. but for the present times, these are inadequate, and to know these is necessary, the sect having witnessed vast changes in times and conditions after 1947 or so. The Princely States which had been giving liberal endowments to the Nātha *āsanas* and monasteries, in some cases since the 14th century or even earlier, are no more and many of the most important monasteries, such as at Tillā in the Salt Ranges and those at Peshawar and in Punjab and Sindh are now in Pakistan while some are in Afghanistan, and their existence, condition and relationship with the *Bārah-Bheka*, the Central Body of the Nāthas, or with Gorakhpur, needs to be ascertained. Moreover there have been vast changes in the lives and outlook of the people in India and their attitude towards religious sects and monasteries, bringing about a marked shift in their interests and values. For these reasons it has been decided to bring out Part I when this lacuna has been removed which will also enable us to know if any hiatus exists in the theory and practice of the *sampradāya*, as suspected by some scholars.

The Sanskrit terms have mostly been given in the present work in their original form along with their English equivalents within brackets. This may be found more advantageous as the English translation of many terms conveys only approximate meaning. A few inadvertent omissions of diacritical marks may be noticed. These will be rectified later when incorporating the suggestions of the learned readers to make the work more useful and error free.

My acknowledgement of gratitude to the earlier scholars whose works are directly or indirectly related to the subject need to be specific. Prof. P.C. Bagchi's edited work "*Kaula-jñāna-nirṇaya*" has been extremely useful for Matsyendranāth's philosophy. In Dr. Kalyani Mallik's book we get a number of important texts relating to the *Nātha Sampradāya* including *Siddha-siddhānta-paddhati*, which has been the main source for the present work. M.M. Gopinath Kaviraj's several scholarly works, though difficult to follow, throw important light on several points, such as, *chakras*, concept of *Kuṇḍalinī, prāṇa*, etc. George Weston Briggs' work is indispensable for anyone working on the *Nātha Sampradāya*. The learned commentary of *Siddha-Siddhānta-Paddhati* in Hindi in the two issues of *Bhāratī*, a Sanskrit journal published from Jaipur, has been invaluable. Dr. A.K. Banerji's work on Gorakshanātha's philosophy has been very useful in elucidation of several terms in the first two chapters dealing with the evolution of the Universe. M.M. P.V. Kane's *History of the Dharma-Śāstra* has been particularly helpful in the chapter on the *Ashṭāṅga-Yoga* and so also Swami Vivekānand's commentary on the *Yoga-Sūtra*. Jaidev Singh's *Śiva-Sūtras* (tr.) serves as a model of accurate and painstaking study and has been a useful guide. The works of Sir John Woodroffe and Oscar Marcel Hinze have been useful in understanding and interpreting from new angles the *chakras* and the ascent and descent of *Kuṇḍalinī*. The names of other scholars and their valuable works have been duly acknowledged in the text and the references.

I am deeply indebted to the late Prof. G.C. Pande who first asked me to work on this topic and kindly provided me with the opportunity to work at I.I.A.S., Shimla. I also feel highly obliged to Professor Hira Lal Maheshwari, formerly in the Department of Hindi, University of Rajasthan, Jaipur, for lending me many books relating to the Nātha Sampradāya from his personal Library. I am also grateful to my fellow colleagues at the Institute, specially Prof. S.C. Pande, Prof. V.K. Vashishtha and Dr. Neelima Vashishta for their gracious and friendly support, and to Shri Maganlal Verma, former Dy. Registrar, M.D.S. University, Ajmer, for overseeing the typing of the manuscript.

In the end, I wish to express my sincere gratitude to Shri Aditya Goel of Aditya Prakashan, Delhi, for undertaking the publication of this work and bringing it out in a short time.

V.S. Bhatngar,

Jaipur
27.10.2011.

Chapter I

Evolution of *Para-Piṇḍa*, *Anādi-Piṇḍa*, *Ādya-Piṇḍa* and *Pañchabhautika-Jagata*

(Manifestation of the Supreme Spiritual Body of the Supreme Reality and Evolution of the World process)

In *Siddha-Siddhānṭa-Paddhati*, Gorakhanātha describes the evolution of the *Para-Piṇḍa* i.e. *Piṇḍa* of *saguṇa sākāra* Parameśvara, *saguṇa* because it has attributes, and *sākāra* because the universe, the phenomenal creation, is His manifestation which results from self-unfolding of the *Śakti* which inheres in Him.

He says that before the creation of *sṛishṭi*, there is no doer nor any cause in the absence of any active pursuit of an object, neither *Kula* nor *Akula,* and the *Para-Brahma Parameśvara* is unmanifested, and without any name. He is *Anādi Siddha*, eternal, realisable by one's own experience — His *Nijā-Śakti*, which is of the nature of Pure Will, completely indistinguishable from Him, being immanent in Him.[1]

By the mere will of *Para-Brahman* or Parama Śiva to create, says Goraksha, *Parā-Śakti*, which inheres in Him, causes Divine pulsation in *Para-Brahman* and activates *Aparā-Śakti*. This *Aparā-Śakti* assists in the creation of *sṛishṭi*. From that *Aparā-Śakti* evolves I-ness (that I can create the *sṛishṭi*) in *Para-Brahman*. One pure I-ness pervades the entire subtly agitated dynamic consciousness. The *Divine Śakti* is at this stage called *Sūkśmā-Śakti* or *Vimarśa-Śakti* of the Supreme Spirit. At this stage, the Divine I-consciousness of

[1] *Siddha-siddhānta-paddhati* (*SSP*), I.4-5.

the Supreme Spirit or Brahman now perceives His true nature, His non-duality, omnipotence, omniscience, self-determining, with inherent Power of self-reflection. At the fifth stage manifests *Kuṇḍalinī-Śakti*, This is the *Śakti-chakra-krama*, says Goraksha, which leads to the emergence of *Para-Piṇḍa*.[2]

Here we may note that Gorakshanātha clearly maintains that the Supreme Spirit through His own Śakti which inheres in Him creates the universe. Commenting on a Patañjali's *sūtra* (I.24) wherein it is said that the "Īśvara (the Supreme Ruler) is a special *Purusha* untouched by misery, action, their results, and diseases", Vivekānand says that though *Patañjala-Yoga* philosophy is based upon the Sāṃkhya philosophy, "in the latter (Sāṃkhya) there is no place for God, while with the *Yogīs*, God has a place. The *Yogīs*, however, do not mention many ideas about God, such as creating. God as the Creator of the universe is not meant by the Īśvara of the *Yogīs*".[3] In contrast, we note, Gorakshanātha firmly believes in the role of the Supreme Power in the creation of *sṛishṭi*. He rejects "the Non-dualism of the extreme Vedāntists as well as pure Dualism of the *Dvaita-vādis* and pure Pluralism of the *Bahupadārtha-vādīs*" and also "the doctrine of the plurality of unrelated material units or *paramāṇus* integrated and dis-integrated by external causes. The non-dual Spirit", continues Banerji "is to him embodied with His own *Śakti* which is non-different from Him. The Absolute Reality is therefore neither purely non-dual nor purely dual nor plural".[4]

After describing the five stages of the self-unfoldment of the Divine *Śakti* or the five stages of Her self-manifestation, Gorakshanātha mentions the characteristics of each stage in

---

[2] *Ibid.*, I.6-8. "It is the *svabhāva* or very nature of ultimate Reality to manifest" and universe is "simply an opening out (*unmesha*) or expansion (*prasāra*) of the Supreme as Śakti. (*Siva-Sūtras*, Intro. XXI, XXII).

[3] *Yoga-Sūtra*, I.24; *Rāja-Yoga*, pp.138-139.

[4] Philosophy of Gorakhnath (*PGN*), p.92-93.

terms of its five *guṇas* or attributes. According to him, the *Nijā-Śakti* has the following attributes:

1. *Nityatā* i.e. eternally present in the nature of *Para-Brahman.*
2. *Nirañjanatā* (absolutely pure).
3. *Nishpaṅdatā* (without any pulsation implying that there is yet no urge for self-expression in Her nature).
4. *Nirābhāsatā* (differenceless, completely identified with Śiva and not yet distinguishable from Him).
5. *Nirutthānatā* (non-different from Śiva and as yet unaware of Her role in the creation).

At this stage of the gradual unfoldment of the Divine *Śakti* She is not distinguishable from Śiva. "This is *Parā-saṃvit*" says Banerji.[5]

Parā-Śakti, says Goraksha, remains immanent in Parameśvara Śiva, before the creation. Its five attributes are:

1. *Astitā* i.e. at this stage, *Śakti*'s existence becomes a reality.
2. *Aprameyatā* (immeasurable, beyond all determinations and limitations).
3. *Abhinnatā* (not differentiated from the Supreme Spirit, the Paramātman).
4. *Anantatā* (i.e. capable of manifesting Herself in infinite ways).
5. *Avyaktatā* (Her infinite power till this stage remains unmanifested).[6]

At the second stage of the self-unfoldment of the Divine *Śakti*, "there arises within *Nijā-Śakti* a very subtle tendency to activate Herself to unfold Her dynamic character". At this

[5] *SSP*, I.10; *PGN*, p.81.

[6] *SSP*, I.11. Parā-Śakti is just the beginning of the self unfoldment of the Nijā-Śakti or Divine Will.

stage She is called *Parā-Śakti* which is "the first slightly unfolded form of the eternal *Nijā-Śakti*" of Parama Śiva, the Supreme Spirit, whose creative will is at this stage, though as yet unmanifested ... is tending towards manifestation".[7]

As has been observed, the evolution of the universe is due to emerging of *ichchā* in Śiva to create which causes gradual unfoldment of His Śakti.[8]

The five attributes of *Aparā-Śakti,* which marks the third stage of the self-unfoldment of *Nijā-Śakti* or Divine Will, a step forward towards Her self-manifestation at the phenomenal plane, are:

1. *Sphuratā* (inner movement or throbbing for self-expression)
2. *Sphuṭatā* (self expression, to burst into view)
3. *Sphāratā* (widely diffused, throbbing in *Śakti* for self-unfoldment).
4. *Sphoṭatā* (seeking to burst, expand)
5. *Sphūrtitā* (It lends support in the creation of *srishṭi*).[9]

Thus we note that at the third stage arises "some sort of vibration or internal agitation" in the *Parā-Śakti*, there develops some throbbing in *Śakti*, "some push for self-manifestation".

The emergence of *Sūkshmā-Śakti* or *Vimarśa-Śakti* marks the fourth stage of the self-unfoldment of *Nijā-Śakti*: At this stage "one pure I-ness pervades the entire subtly agitated dynamic consciousness". The five *guṇas* of *Sūkshmā-Śakti* are:

1. *Niraṃśatā* (Divine I-consciousness without any duality)
2. *Nirantaratā* (continuity in I-consciousness of the Śakti)

---

[7] *PGN*, p.82.

[8] *Tāntrika-Sādhanā aur Siddhānta*, pp.210-11.

[9] *SSP*, I.12.

3. *Niśchalatā* (calm and stable i.e. there is no increase or decrease in the intensity of the urge for self unfoldment).
4. *Niśchayatā* (Free from all kinds of uncertainties and delusions and "perfect certitude or fullness of self knowledge").
5. *Nirvikalpatā* (Divine self-knowledge).[10]

At this stage, as has been nicely put, the Supreme Spirit has now "the delightful self-experience as the absolute Divine Personality without any duality, limitation, imperfection, doubt or uncertainty or incompleteness with regard to the experience. .... He now perceives His non-duality, omnipotence and omniscience, His infinite and perfect existence ..." As Shri Jaideva Singh in his introduction to the *Śiva-Sūtras* says, "This *Vimarśa* is *svātantrya* or unimpeded sovereign power or *Śakti* .... It contains all that is to be" and quotes *Parātriṁśikā*, which says, "As the great banyan tree lies only in the form of potency in the seed, even so the entire universe with all the mobile and immobile beings lies as a potency in the heart of the Supreme".[11]

At the fifth stage, *Nijā-Śakti* emerges as "a distinct Psychic Power", *Kunḍalinī*, eternal "with infinite possibilities of self-manifestation, self-diversification, self-transformation" and the five attributes (guṇa) of *Kunḍalinī-Śakti* are:

1. *Pūrṇatā* (fullness, completeness, *nitya*, indivisible)
2. *Pratibimbatā* (After penetrating the nine *chakras*, this *Mahāśakti* is reflected in the body of the *Yogī* like *Jyoti*).
3. *Prabalatā* (omnipotent, endowed with *Mahā Śakti,* which has "unlimited power for creating from within Herself varius orders of existences".)
4. *Prochchalatā* (inherent self-transforming character)

---

[10] *Ibid*, I.13.

[11] *PGN*, p.85; *Śiva-Sūtras*, Intr. XXI; *Parātriṁśikā*, 34.

5. *Pratyaṅg-mukhatā* (ever present yearning for creation of *sṛishṭi*).[12]

In this way, *Para-Piṇḍa* inhering the five attributes or *guṇas* of each of five *Śaktis*, viz., *Nijā-Śakti, Parā-Śakti, Aparā-Śakti*, *Sūkshmā-Śakti* and *Kuṇḍalinī-Śakti* emerges, in the manner called *Śakti-chakra-krama* as a result of which Sadā Śiva emerges in five forms,[13] says *Siddha-Siddhānta-Paddhati.* As Banerji writes, "Within the self-consciousness of *Para-Piṇḍa* all forms and all stages of consciousness are most wonderfully harmonised and unified. He is the Supreme Divinity comprising all Divinities".[14]

II

Five *tattvas* and 25 *guṇas* of *Anādi-Piṇḍa*

In the evolution of the Cosmic Body, *Siddha-Siddhānta-Paddhati (SSP),* first gives the five *tattvas* and twenty-five *guṇas* (attributes) of *Anādya-Piṇḍa* "the uncreated and all-creating Divine Personality" existing since eternity.

The five *tattvas* are:

1. *Aparampara* (presiding deity, Sadā Śiva governing *Nijā-Śakti*)
2. *Paramapada* (presiding *Deva* is Parameśvara, *adhishṭhātā* of *Parā-Śakti*)
3. *Śūnya* (Presiding *deva* Rudra, *adhishṭhātā* of *Aparā Śakti*)
4. *Nirañjana* (Presiding deity Vishṇu, governing *Sūkshmā-Śakti*)
5. *Paramātmā* (the creator of the Universe).[15]

Now from *Aparampara* emanates *sphurtā* or Divine Pulsation, *bhāvanā* from *Paramapada* (Parameśvara), from

---

[12] *SSP*, I.14.
[13] *SSP*, I.15-16.
[14] *PGN*, p.93.
[15] *SSP*, I.17.

Śūnya emanates *sva-sattāmātra*, from *Nirañjana sva-sākshātakāra-mātra* i.e. *ahaṃkāra*, and from *Paramātmā* emanates *samashṭi pinḍa* useful in the creation of the *sṛishṭi*.[16]

The five *guṇas* or attributes of each of the five *tattvas* of *Anādi-Pinḍa* are described in the following manner in *Siddha-Siddhānta-Paddhati* by Gorkshanātha. Thus *Aparampara* (Sadā Śiva) has five *guṇas* (attributes):

1. *Akalaṅkatva* (free from any defect)
2. *Anupamatva* (without equal, unique)
3. *Aparātva* (infinite, eternal)
4. *Amūrtatva* (unembodied)
5. *Anudayatva* (without *Prāgabhāva, Prāga* meaning prior existence i.e. beyond birth or dissolution.[17]

The five *guṇas* of *Paramapada* (Parameśvara) are:

1. *Nishkala* (*Nirākāra*, without any form)
2. *Aṇu* (smaller than *aṇu* or atom)
3. *Achala* (immovable, name of Śiva)
4. *Asaṃkhya* (limitless)
5. *Nirādhāra* (Self-sustainable).[18]

The five *guṇas* or attributes of *Śūnya* are:

1. *Līnatā* (state of being non-manifest)
2. *Pūrṇatā* (Perfection, *akhaṇḍatā*)
3. *Unmanī* (highest state of consciousness)
4. *Lolatā* (tremulousness)
5. *Mūrchchā* (dissolution in *Mahā Pralaya*).[19]

The five *guṇas* or attributes of *Nirañjana* are:

1. *Satyatva* (free from error)
2. *Sahajatva* (not subject to any change)

---

16 *Ibid*, I.18.
17 *Ibid.*, I.19.
18 *Ibid.*, I.20.
19 *Ibid.*, I.21.

3. *Samarastva* (having the same consciousness, identical)
4. *Sāvadhānatā* (attentive)
5. *Sarvagatatva* (power to go any where).[20]

The five *guṇas* of Paramātmā or Universal Soul:

1. *Akshayatva* (undecaying)
2. *Abhedyatā* (impenetrability)
3. *Achchedyatā* (indivisibility)
4. *Avināśitva* (imperishability)
5. *Adāhyātva* (incombustibility).[21]

At the time of *Mahā Pralaya*, says Gorakshanātha, the entire universe undergoes dissolution in the *Mahā-Śakti*, which remains completely non-different from *Chidrūpa Parameśvra*, the Supreme Being. At the time of creation, the five *Mahā-Śaktis*, each with the five attributes, become manifest.

The *Chetana* (*Parama Śiva* or transcendent Śiva) with His five *Mahā-śaktis*, and five *tattvas* viz. *Aparampara, Parampada, Śūnya, Nirañjana* and *Parmātamā* form *Anādya Piṇḍa*.

The commentator of *SSP* writes, "This is verily Sachchidānanda Parameśvara which manifests with the above mentioned twenty-five attributes, five each of its five *tattvas*. This *Samashṭi-Deva* is Parameśvara Śiva".[22]

III

Manifestation of *Ādya-Piṇḍa-Purusha* from *Anādya-Piṇḍa Parameśvara*:

From *Anādya-Piṇḍa-Parmeśvara* emanates *Ādya-Piṇḍa-Purusha,* says Goraksha, which is the First Cosmic Personality

---

[20] *Ibid.*, I.22.

[21] *Ibid.*, I.23.

[22] *Ibid.*, I.24; *Bhāratī*, I, p.21.

of Śiva and inheres the *svarūpa* of *Parmānanda, Prabodha, Chidudaya Chitprakāśa* and *Ahaṃ-bhāva*. These manifest in the following order:

From *Anādya-Piṇḍa* emanates *Parmānanda*, from *Parmānanda* emanates *Prabodha*, from *Prabodha* appears *Chidudaya*, from *Chidudaya* comes *Chitprakāśa* and from *Chitprakāśa* comes *Ahaṃ-bhāva*.[23] The main five attributes of each of these five are thus given by Goraksha in *SSP*:

The five *guṇas* or attributes of *Parmānanda* are:

1. *Spanda* (pulsation or agitation in the consciousness)
2. *Harsha* (delight, thrilling sensation or delightful wonder)
3. *Utsāha* (enthusiasm)
4. *Nishpanda* (perfect calmness)
5. *Nitya Sukhatva* ("unemotional enjoyment of eternal bliss within").[24]

The five *guṇas* of *Prabodha* which implies "as it were a new phenomenal awakening in His transcendent self-conscious nature" are:

1. *Udaya* ("rising of consciousness above the horizon of the perfectly tranquil non-differentiated state")
2. *Ullāsa* (keenness for self-manifestation).
3. *Avabhāsa* (consciousness of His spiritual nature)
4. *Vikāsa* (experience of the self-evolution of His *Śakti*)
5. *Prabhā* ("shedding lusture upon all aspects of His all pervading existence").[25]

The five attributes of *Chid-udaya* are:

1. *Sadbhāva*
2. *Vichāra*

---

[23] *SSP*, I.25.

[24] *Ibid.*, I.26.

[25] *Ibid.*, I.27.

3. *Kartṛitva*
4. *Jñātṛitva*
5. *Svatantratva*.[26]

These have been explained by Banerji in the following manner: By *Chid-udaya*, writes Banerji (pp.95-96), "Gorakhnātha means the self-manifestation of the Transcendent Consciousness as the self-knowing and all-knowing, self-reflecting and all-reflecting, self-determining and all-determining, Conscious Subject". He characterizes this aspect of the Divine Personality by such attributes, as *Sadbhāva* i.e. "Spirit's clear knowledge of Himself as the sole Reality", *Vichāra* i.e. His reflection upon Himself as the source and Centre of all possible phenomenal realities, *Karṭritva* or His consciousness of Himself as the Source of all possible actions, *Jñātritva* i.e. His consciousness of Himself as the Knower of objects, and *Swatantratva* i.e. His consciousness of Himself as perfectly free or governed by His own Laws.[27]

The five *guṇas* of *Chitprakāśa* are:

1. *Nirvikāratva* (Free from changes of form or nature)
2. *Nishkalatva* ("freedom from any sense of partition within Himself")
3. *Nirvikalpatva* (Free from all thought-constructs)
4. *Samatā* ("complete identity or oneness with His consciousness")
5. *Viśrānti* (cessation of all *chitta-vṛittis*),[28]

The five *guṇas* or attributes of *So-haṃ bhāva* are:

1. *Ahaṃtā* (feeling of being omnipresent)
2. *Akhaṇḍa Aiśvarya* (feeling of undivided, unlimited power and prosperity)

[26] *Ibid.*, I.28.
[27] *PGN*, pp.95-96.
[28] *SSP*, I.29.

3. *Svātmatā* (to feel that "all His *aisvarya* is non-different from Himself")
4. *Viśvānubhava Sāmarthya* (power to manifest all things — subtle as well as gross)
5. *Sarvajñatva* (omniscient).[29]

As noted, *Ādya-Piṇḍa*, which is the Cosmic Body of Śiva, is said to inhere all these five, viz. *Parmānanda, Prabodha, Chid-udaya, Chitprakāśa* and *Ahaṃbhāva*, which in this order emanate from *Anādya-Piṇḍa.*

One may find the conception of *Ādya-Piṇḍa* to correspond to the conception of Hiraṇyagarbha of the *Veda*. It is proclaimed in *Ṛigveda*, writes Banerji that "the Divine Personality with the entire cosmic order in an ideal form in His womb manifested Himself first of all and He became by nature the sole Lord of all existences. .... It is also said that He is the First Embodied Being, and He is called the Person (i.e. the Divine Personality). He is spoken of as *Saguna Brahma* ..."[30]

In Kashmir Śaivism, the creative aspect of Parama Śiva, known as *Śiva tattva* is described in this manner:

1. *Śiva tattva* which is "the initial creative movement or *prathama spanda* of Parama Śiva".
2. *Śakti tattva* is "the Energy of Śiva which polarizes Consciousness into *Ahaṃ* and *Idam* (I and This)", is not separate from Śiva, and is His "creative aspect", His *ahaṁvimarśa* (I-consciousness), His *unmuukhtā* or intentness to create, as the learned translator of the *Śiva-Sūtras* says. "In *Śakti tattva, ānanda* aspect is predominant. The Parama Śiva pours out the delightful wonder of his splendour into manifestation".
3. *Sadāśiva tattva* is the will (*Ichchā*) of the Parama Śiva

[29] *SSP*, I.30.
[30] *PGN*, p.97.

to affirm "I am This" but 'This' is only a hazy (*ashpuṭa*) experience ... The Ideal Universe is experienced, as an indistinct something in the depth of Consciousness".

4. *Īśvara Tattava:* At this stage, *Idam*, or 'This side of the total experience becomes a little more defined (*sphuṭa*). It is *unmesha* or distinct blossoming of the Universe". At this stage *jñāna* or knowledge is predominant'.
5. *Sadvidyā Tattva:* At this stage "the 'I' and the 'This' side of the experience are equally balanced. .... and the *svarupa* or the real nature is not yet veiled".

It is after this stage that *Māyā tattva* begins to veil the Divine with the help of the five *Kañchukas* or coverings — *Kalā, Vidyā, Rāga, Kāla* and *Niyati*.[31] One may note that the basic concepts in the above account closely resemble those we have discussed earlier in the description of the emergence of the *Ādya-Piṇḍa*.

Evolution of the physical universe (*Pañcha-bhautika-Jagat*)

The whole universe with all the laws which maintain it in a subtle form exists in the *Ādya-Piṇḍa* which with further unfoldment of His *Śakti* is now manifested in grosser and grosser physical forms. Like all important systems of Indian philosophy, Gorakhanātha conceives this physical universe as constituted of five Great elements or *Mahā-Bhūtas*. As Baneraji says, "The universe which was ideally real in the nature of *Ādya-Piṇḍa* becomes physically and objectively real as the Cosmic Body of Śiva or *Mahā-Sākāra-Piṇḍa*, a form of self-manifestation of the *Mahā Śakti* of Śiva. Śiva .... with His infinite and eternal *Mahā Śakti* is immanent in all diversities of this physical order". He regards this conception of the

[31] *Śiva-Sūtras*, XXII-XXIV.

physical universe as the Cosmic Body of Śiva as a "most magnificent idea of the philosophy of *Siddha Yogīs*".[32]

As has been pointed out, the Vedāntists regard the world of *Mahābhūtas* as having only illusory existence "born of *Māyā* or *Avidyā* and the Supreme Spirit, Brahman, as substratum (*adhishṭhāna*) of this illusion", whereas Gorakshanātha and other *Mahā Yogīs* regard the world's observable to us as a "self-manifestation and embodiment of the Supreme Spirit, by virtue of the real Power (*Śakti*) inherent in this Spirit". According to Śāṃkhya, the *Pañcha-Mahābhūtas* have evolved from *Pañcha-Tanmātrās* which have evolved from *Ahaṃ-tattva* (One Ego Principle) which has evolved from *Mahat-tattva*, "the first manifestation (*vyakta-rūpa*) of *Mūla Prakṛiti* or *Ayakta tattva*". According to Sāṃkhya, the *Mahābhūtas* are not "ultimate realities though they are ultimate material constituents of the objective world, which is not created by or evolved from any Supreme Spirit or Īśvara, but as evolved from *Mūla Prakṛiti* ... without any supervision and control of any eternal Supreme Lord of this *Prakṛiti*". The views of the *Mahā Yogīs* regarding the origin of the *Pañcha-Mahābhūtas* from the Supreme Spirit is closely similar to what *Taittirīya Upanishad* says, "From that Supreme Spirit (Brahman), who is also *Ātmā* or the True Self of every thing, *Ākāśa* is born. From *Ākāśa Vāyu* is evolved, from *Vāyu Agni*, from *Agni Ap*, and from *Ap Pṛithvī*". [33]

Coming back to Gorakshanātha's version of the evolution of the *Pañcha-Mahābhūtas* in detail, he says that from the *Ādya Piṇḍa*, evolves *Mahā-Ākāśa* from which comes forth *Mahā-vāyu*. From *Mahā-Vāyu* comes *Mahā-Teja* (Agni), from which comes forth *Mahā-Salila* and from *Mahā-Salila* appears *Mahā-Pṛithvī*. Thus the five *Bhūtas* or physical elements evolve one after the other from *Ādya Piṇḍa*.[34]

---

32 *PGN*, p.100.

33 *PGN*, pp109-11.

34 *SSP*, I. vs.31; Cf. *Śārīrika Upanishad*, 113-114 in *Thirty Minor Upanishads* (Tr. K.N. Aiyar)

Each of these five *Mahā-Bhūtas*, or *Mahātattvas* says *SSP*, has five (main) attributes or *guṇa* as described below:

The five *guṇas* (attributes) of *Mahā-Ākāśa* are:

1. *Avakāśa* (in its vast expanse, all things can find shelter)
2. *Achchidratva* (without an opening or hole)
3. *Asprasatva* (cannot be touched being *asaṅga* and is not affected by changes which take place in realities "which evolve from and within it")
4. *Nīlavarṇatva* (in appearance blue or blue-colouredness though in reality Ākāśa has no visible property)
5. *Śabdatva* (the quality of full of *śabda* which may be in any of the four stages — *Parā, Paśyantī, Madhyamā* and *Vaikharī*).[35]

Mahā-Ākaśa is the first self-manifestation of Śiva-Śakti in this cosmic order.

The five *guṇas* (attributes) of *Mahā-Vāyu*:

1. *Saṃchāra* (possessed with quality of motion)
2. *Saṃchālana* (having quality of motion and of causing movement)
3. *Sparśa* (touches all material objects)
4. *Soshaṇa* (*Vāyu* has the quality of absorbing "particular or qualities of other grosser elements evolved from it" such as heat of *agni*, coldness of *salila*, without destroying them.
5. *Dhūmra-varṇatva* (of the colour of *dhūmra* or smoke colouredness).[36]

Vāyu represents the second stage of the self-unfoldment of the Divine Energy. *Ākāśa* and *Vāyu* are "the first two primary

[35] *SSP*, I.32.

[36] *Ibid.*, I.33.

constituents of the *Mahā-sākāra-pinḍa* i.e. the objective physical universe".

Mahā-Teja: Its five *guṇas* or five essential attributes are:

1. *Dāhakatva* (quality of burning or combustion)
2. *Pāchakatva* (quality of assimilation)
3. *Ūshṇatva* (heat)
4. *Prakāśa* (Light. It manifests various things)
5. *Rakta-varṇatva* (of red colour).[37]

The five essential attributes of *Mahā-Salila* are:

1. *Pravāha* (continuous flow)
2. *Āpyāyana* (coming from water)
3. *Dṛva* (fluidity)
4. *Rasa* (palatableness)
5. *Śveta-Varṇatva* (of white colour).[38]

It has been pointed out that *Mahā-salila* should not be taken to mean the gross water of our common experience. "It is the soothing *Drav-rūpa* (Fluid Body) of Śiva-Śakti".[39] The five essential attributes of *Mahā-Pṛithvī* are:

1. *Sthūlatā* (gross)
2. *Nānākārtā* (of innumerable variety, diversity)
3. *Kāṭhinya* (hardness)
4. *Gandha* (aroma)
5. *Pīta-varṇatva* (yellow coloured).

Mahā-Pṛithvī is the "grossest and most condensed form of physical self-manifestation of Śiva-Śakti". [40]

The above are "the ultimate constituents of the physical universe which is conceived as *Mahā-Sakāra-Pinḍa* of Śiva-Śakti — the *sthūla mūrti* of Śiva-Śakti.

---

[37] *Ibid.*, I.34.

[38] *Ibid.*, I.35.

[39] *PGN*, p.106.

[40] *Ibid.*, I.36; *PGN*, p.106.

Ashṭa-mūrti of Mahāsākāra-Pinḍa Śiva

The eight Divine self manifestations of Mahāsākāra-Pinḍa Śiva, each manifesting from the preceding one, are Śiva, Bhairava, Śri Kanṭha, Sadā Śiva, Iśvara, Rudra, Vishṇu and Brahmā. The tasks of creation, maintenance and destruction are performed through them. One crosses the Ocean of existence by Their grace, and hence they are the object of worship and veneration, says Gorakshanātha.

As A.K. Banerji says, they are not different from Śiva, and the same Divine Power operates in all these manifestations of Śiva. "It is in the light of the different kinds of self-manifestation of one Śakti of Śiva that different powers, qualities and functions are associated with these names". Thus Brahmā, Vishṇu and Rudra are associated with "the cosmic functions of Creation, Preservation and Destruction which are equally important for the continuity and ever-newness of this spatio-temporal order. .... Creation is the process of diversification and destruction is the process of unification (as individual bodies are destroyed and then resolved into their constituent elements). All these processes are continuous in the Cosmic Body of Śiva", he says.[41]

---

[41] *SSP*, I.37; *PGN*, p113.

Chapter II

Creation of Gross Material Body (*Prakṛiti-Piṇḍa* or human body) and Factors which influence Man's nature, mind and forms of Self Expression

Gorakshanātha describes the human organism as consisting of (1) gross material body (*Bhūta-piṇḍa*), (2) the Mental body or *Antaḥkaraṇa-pañchaka*, (3) Factors which influence man's nature, mind, actions (*kula-pañchaka* or fivefold *kula*), (4) *Vyakti-Pañchaka* or five forms of self-expression of individual mind, (5) Fivefold perceptible determinant causes of acquiring this perishable body (*Pratyakshakaraṇa-Pañchaka*) and (6) the system of *Nāḍis* and ten *Prāṇā-vāyu*. He thus takes a very comprehensive view of the nature of human body.

Creation of *Prakṛiti-Piṇḍa* in the form of human body and twenty-five attributes of the *Pañcha-Bhūtas* are given in *Siddha-Siddhānta-Paddhati* as under:

Prakṛiti-Piṇḍa is called *Pañchabhautika-Śarīra* as it is formed of five *Bhūtas*, each of which has five attributes (*guṇa*). The five *Bhūtas* are *Pṛithivī tattva, Jala tattva, Teja (Agni) tattva, Vāyu tattva* and *Ākāśa tattva* which appear more prominently in different parts of the human body.[1] The *guṇas* (attributes) of each of these *tattvas* of materiality have been described briefly as follows:

The five *guṇas* of *Pṛithivī tattva* in this *Pañchabhautika-śarīra* are the following:

---

[1] *Siddha-siddhānta-paddhati* (*SSP*), I.38.

1. *Asthi* (bones)
2. *Māns* (flesh)
3. *Tvachā* (skin)
4. *Nāḍī* (veins and arteries)
5. *Roma* (hair on the body)[2]

Pṛithvī tattva appears more prominently than others in the above *guṇas* of the human organism,

And the five *guṇas* of *Jala tattva* in this physical body are:

1. Lāra (saliva)
2. *Mūtra* (urine)
3. *Śukra* (semen)
4. *Śoṇita* (blood)
5. *Sveda* (perspiration).[3]

In these liquid substances of the body, *Jala* or *Salila* is more conspicuous.

The five attributes of *Teja tattva* are:

1. *Kshudhā* (hunger)
2. *Tṛishā* (strong desire)
3. *Nidrā* (sleep)
4. *Kānti* (brightness)
5. *Ālasya* (lassitude).[4]

In the above five attributes of *Tejās*, Agni's manifestation is conspicuous.

The five guṅas of *Vāyu tattva* are:

1. *Dhāvana* (motion)
2. *Bhramaṇa* (roaming about, circumbutating)
3. *Prasāraṇa* (spreading out)
4. *Ākuñchana* (capacity to bend)
5. *Nirodha* (to hold back or check).[5]

---

[2] *Ibid*, I.39.
[3] *Ibid.*, I.40.
[4] *Ibid.*, I.41.

These are chiefly determined by the *Vāyu* element.

And the five attributes of *Ākāśa tattva* are:

1. *Rāga* (attachment)
2. *Dvesha* (dislike, enmity)
3. *Bhaya* (fear)
4. *Lajjā* (shame)
5. *Moha* (delusion),[6]

These are "the special manifestations" of the element *Ākāśa*. It is these attributes of *Ākāśa tattva* that give rise to feelings of antagonism and discord.

Having thus described the five gross *bhūtas* (each possessing five *guṇas*), which constitute the gross physical body, Gorakshanātha describes the *tattvas* of mental operation. The commentator of SSP, writes that these are the very nature of *antaḥakaraṇa* (inner psychic apparatus).[7]

II

Analysis of the nature of Mind (evolution of the mental body)

This physical body is driven or controlled by five *vṛittis* of the psychic apparatus of the individual or *Antaḥkaraṇa*. These are *Mana, Buddhi, Ahaṃkāra, Chitta* and *Chaitanya*, each of which has five attributes or *guṇas*.[8]

The five *guṇas* of *Mana* (empirical mind) are:

1. *Saṃkalpa* (desire or will)
2. *Vikalpa* (doubt and uncertainty in mind)
3. *Mūrchchā* (temporary state of blank-mindness or senselessness)
4. *Jaḍatā* (lack of *viveka*, confused thinking)
5. *Manana* (reflection).[9]

---

[5] *Ibid*, I.42.

[6] *Ibid*, I.43.

[7] *Ibid.*, I.44.

[8] *Ibid.*

[9] *Ibid.*, I.45.

And five *guṇas* or attributes of *Buddhi* or ascertaining intelligence are manifested as:

1. *Viveka* (discrimination, ability to see the reality)
2. *Vairāgya* (non-attachment, freedom from all objects, desires; asceticism)
3. *Śānti* (mental peace)
4. *Santosha* (contentment)
5. *Kshamā* (forgiveness).[10]

All these five attributes are closely related with one another. *Viveka* or capacity to recognize the Reality develops *vairāgya* or non-attachment, which gives peace and ends unsteadiness of mind. *Viveka, vairāgya* and *śānti* lead to *santosha* or contentment. The mind becomes restful, all cravings end and the mind now habitually abides in *Ātma-svarūpa*. This creates a strong tendency to be charitable and forgiving.[11] The objects that are reflected in *Buddhi* are said to be of two kinds (1) external, which are perceived through the eyes and (2) internal "impressions left behind in the mind".[12]

The five *guṇas* or attributes of *Ahaṃkāra* are:

1. *Abhimāna* (ego)
2. *Madīya* (Possessiveness)
3. *Mamasukha* (concern only about one's own happiness)
4. *Mamadukha* (brooding all the time over one's own sorrow)
5. *Mamedam* or *mama-idam* (concerned about one's own interest).[13]

Ahaṃkāra is described as a product of *buddhi*. "It is the I-making principle and the power of self-appropriation".[14]

---

[10] *Ibid.*, I.46.
[11] *Bhāratī*, p.25.
[12] *Śiva-Sūtras*, xxvii.
[13] *SSP*, I.47.
[14] *Śiva-Sūtras*, xxvii.

The five attributes or *guṇas* of *Chitta* are:

1. *Mati* (inclination, disposition)
2. *Dhṛiti* (Patience to conserve energy)
3. *Smṛiti* (*Jñāna* acquired from the *saṁskāras*))
4. *Tyāga* (sacrifice, preparedness to part with one's dearest thing for a deserving cause)
5. *Svīkāra* (to accept something in conformity with the norms).[15]

The five *guṇas* of *Chaitanya* are:

1. *Vimarśa* (rational reflection)
2. *Śīlana* (cultivated self-discipline)
3. *Dhairya* (Patience)
4. *Chintana* (contemplation)
5. *Nihsprahatva* (absence of desires).[16]

The above are the twenty-five attributes of the five *vṛittis* of *Antaḥakaraṇa*, viz., *Mana, Buddhi, Ahaṃkāra, Chitta* and *Chaitanya* or twenty-five forms of manifestation of mind in the individual body. It is in this manner that Gorakshanātha has described the formation of *Sūkshma Śarīra* or subtle body.

In the Śaiva system of Kashmir (*Trika-śāstra*), *manas, buddhi* and *ahaṃkāra*, which constitute *antaḥkraṇa* (psychic apparatus) along with 5 *tanmātras* or primary elements of perception (sound, touch, *rūpa, rasa* or flavour and *gandha* or odour) "form the *sūkshma śarīra* in which the soul leaves the body at the time of death".[17]

III
Kula-Pañchaka

The three *guṇas* viz. *Sattva*, *Rajas* and *Tamas* along with

---

[15] *SSP*, I.48.

[16] *SSP*, I.49.

[17] *Śiva-Sūtras*, Jaideva Singh, Intro.xxix.

Kāla and *Jīva* form the *Pañcha-Kula*. They are principal (*kula*) in the sense that they play an important part in regulating *Bhāva* (disposition), *Mana* or Mind, *Buddhi*, sense-organs, etc.[18]

These five operating together in various ways influence "the evolution of the character of an individual mind in an individual body. They seem to be immanent in the nature of every individual, even from his embryonic state and exert their influence during all the stages of his development". Gorakshanātha has given these *guṇas* the generic name *Kula-Pañchaka*.[19]

The attributes of *Sattva guṇa* are:

1. *Dayā* (kindness towards all living beings)
2. *Dharma* (righteousness)
3. *Kriyā* (good and virtuous acts)
4. *Bhakti* (love and devotion towards the Supreme Spirit, Paramātmā)
5. *Shraddhā* (faith in true knowledge of Self or *ātma-jñāna*).[20]

Sattva guṇa on account of its virtues and purity creates *chetanatā* and develops power of discrimination or *viveka śakti*. *Sattva* is the aspect of harmony, goodness, enlightenment and *sukha* (pleasure) and "inspires the human mind with higher moral and spiritual ideas, and elevates it to higher planes of consciousness".[21]

Describing the five attributes of *Rajoguṅa*, *SSP* says that these are:

1. *Dāna* (charity)
2. *Bhoga* (desire for worldly enjoyments, sensuous and mental)

---

[18] *SSP*, I.50.

[19] *Philosophy of Gorakhnāth (PGN)*, p.146

[20] *SSP*, I.51.

[21] *SSP*, I.51; *PGN*, p.144.

3. *Śṛingāra* (love for decoration, ornaments)
4. *Vastu grahaṇa* (insatiable desire for appropriation of more things)
5. *Svārtha Saṃgrahaṇa* (selfish acquisition).[22]

And the five *vṛittis* of *Tamoguṇa* are:

1. *Vivāda* (needless controversies and argumentation)
2. *Kalaha* (lack of harmony, strife, contention)
3. *Śoka* (grief, sorrow)
4. *Vadha* (does not hesitate to take a violent course)
5. *Vañchana* (tendency to cheat) (SSP, I.53)

Tamoguṇa originates from *ajñāna* (ignorance) and gives rise to *pramāda* (indolence) and tendency to ignore the right path.

And the five attributes of *Kāla* are:

1. *Kalanā* (calculation of figures, number, periods, years etc.)
2. *Kalpanā* (creativity)
3. *Bhrānti* (confusion of thoughts and misunderstanding of facts)
4. *Pramāda* (tendency to be indolent, careless or negligent)
5. *Anartha* (unexpected misfortunes)[23]

All the above factors are in one way or the other related to time (*kāla*) which influences actions, developments and their outcome.

And five *guṇas* or *avasthā* or state of *Jīva* (Individual self) are:

1. *Jāgrata* or waking state.
2. *Svapna* (the state of dream, in which the mind has

---

[22] *Ibid.*, I.52-53.

[23] *Ibid.*, I, 54.

various experiences at the sub-conscious level).

3. *Sushupti* (the state of deep sleep, in which there is total absence of objective consciousness)
4. *Turyāvasthā* (fourth state of consciousness, beyond the state of waking, dreaming and deep sleep)
5. *Turyātīta avasthā* (state of consciousness beyond the *turīya* state, in which the jīva is established in *Nirvikalpa samādhi*).

Turīya is described as "pure chidānand-consciousness and bliss. The individual's mind is conditioned by habit, energy (*vāsnā*) of previous lives. When by Yogic practices, his mind becomes deconditioned, then he attains *turīya* consciousness and becomes *jīvana-mukta* or liberated while still alive".[24]

As mentioned, the three *guṇas* — *Sattva, Rajas, Tamas*, along with *Kāla* and *Jīva* form the *Pañcha-Kula*. In what sense the term *Kula* has been used in *SSP*? According to one view, these are principal in the sense that they play "as invisible determining force" an important part in regulating the nature and character of an individual since they affect his mind, *Bhāva* or disposition, *Buddhi* and sense organs.

In Trika-śāstra (of Kashmīr) *Prakṛiti* is described as having three *guṇas* viz., *sattva, rajas, tamas* which, in her unmanifested state, are held in perfect equipoise. According to *Pratyabhijñā*, "*Prakṛiti* is the *Śāntā Śakti* of Śiva, and the *guṇas sattva, rajas* and *tamas* are only the polarization of His *śaktis* of *jñāna, ichchā* and *kriyā* respectively".[25]

IV

Five forms of self-expression of the Individual mind *(Vyakti Pañchaka)* and their twenty five *guṇas*

The following are the five forms of self-expression of the individual minds as given in *SSP*:

---

[24] *Ibid.*, I, 55; *Śiva-Sūtras*, xxix.

[25] *Śiva-Sūtras*, Intro.xxvii.

1. *Ichchā* or desire
2. *Kriyā* or action
3. *Māyā* (artfulness, pretension)
4. *Prakṛiti* (nature or temperament)
5. *Vāk* (speech)

Their presence in the *Sūkshma Śarīra* (inner subtle body) directs a person's behaviour and conduct.[26] Each of these is expressed in five different forms.

The five attributes of *Ichchā* or its manifestations are:

1. *Unmāda* (wild, insane impulses and excitement when *ichchā* has not been fulfilled).
2. *Vāsanā* (present consciousness of past perception)
3. *Vāñchhā* (longing for wealth and other worldly things, pleasure and power)
4. *Chintā* (planning ways and means to attain an object)
5. *Cheshṭā* (mental effort or resolution for attaining the desired object).[27]

All the above five are at the mental level.

The five attributes or forms of manifestation of *Kriyā* are:

1. *Smaraṇa* (remembrance of the object or purpose to be attained)
2. *Udyoga* (physical effort to attain the objective)
3. *Kārya* (active pursuit of an object)
4. *Niśchaya* (pursuit of an object with firm determination)
5. *Svakulāchāra* (to act in conformity with the norms approved by the *kula*).[28]

As Banerji writes: *Ichchā* and *kriyā* and the other forms of *Vyakti* (*Māyā, Prakṛiti* and *Vāk*) are generally influenced by

[26] *Ibid.*, I, 56.
[27] *Ibid.*, I, 57.
[28] *Ibid.*, I, 58.

the predominance of one or the other of the *Kulas* described earlier, viz., *Sattva, Rajas, Tamas, Kāla* and *Jeeva*, — at any particular period. "This explains why the desires and actions of different individuals are found to be directed towards different kinds of objects, good or bad, and even in the case of the same individual they take different directions at different times or at different stages of the development of his life".[29]

Māyā, according to *SSP*, also manifests in five forms:

1. *Mada* (pride and actions originating from it)
2. *Matsarya* (selfishness, greed, envy and tendencies and actions originating from these).
3. *Dambha* (self-conceited expression of ones position, ability, achievements, hypocrisy, etc.)
4. *Kṛitrimatā* (artificiality, taking recourse to untruth)
5. *Asada Vyavahāra* (false conduct and behaviour).

As all the five forms of manifestations of *Māyā* indicate predominance of *Rajas* and *Tamas guṇas* in the nature of an individual, these need to be overcome "for ascending the higher planes of human personality".[30]

Prakṛiti, which is the nature of *Antaḥkaraṇa* has the following five *guṇas* or attributes:

1. *Āśā* (hope for favourable prospects in future)
2. *Trishṇā* (desire for more and more)
3. *Spṛihā* (desire for objects of enjoyment)
4. *Kānkshā* (ambition)
5. *Mithyā* (entertain false hopes).[31]

Prakṛiti is the fourth kind of self-expression of individual mind and indicates the temperament of an individual.

And five attributes of *Vāk* (speech), which is important for the conduct of the activities of *Antaḥkaraṇa*, the thinking faculty, are:

---

[29] *PGN*, p.147.

[30] *SSP*, I.59.

[31] *Ibid.*, I, 60.

1. *Parā* (urge for self-expression without showing any signs for the same)
2. *Paśyantī* (stage of *Vāk* when manifested at mental stage and not in any sound form)
3. *Madhyamā* (stage between *Paśyantī* and articulate sound-speech)
4. *Vaikharī* (audible spoken words)
5. *Mātṛikā* (ultimate phonetic constituents of Vaikharī Vāk).[32]

The *śabda* is made of *Varṇas*. The four stages of this *śabda* (*parā, paśyantī, madhyamā* and vaikharı) or of the genesis of sounds "correspond with the four stages of the development of the formless thought into the concrete idea also represent the four stages in the process of receiving a sound".[33]

These are the five *rūpa* of *vāk*. The first, *parā*, is said to reside in the *Mūlādhāra chakra* and is experienced by a *yogī* in the state of *Nirvikalpa Samādhi*. The second is *paśyantī* The *Parāvākparāvāṇī* on reaching the navel region acquires a gross form which is called *Paśyantī vāṇī* which the *yogī* realizes in *Savikalpa Samādhi*. Third *rūpa* of *vāk* is *Madhyamā* which is acquired when *Paśyantī vāṇī* enters the heart region. When the *vāṇī* after returning from the head reaches the throat then the *śabda* resulting from it called *Vaikharī vānī* which is the fourth *rūpa* of *vāk*. The fifth is *Mātṛikā varṇa* (root-letters) which, according to the ***Siddha*** *yogīs* and Tāntrika schools are not merely "the ultimate constituents of articulate speech .... Each letter is a particularized sound-embodiment of Śiva-Śakti ... surcharged with a vital force and a spiritual meaning" and to indicate Śiva aspect and Śakti aspect in these root-letters (*Mātṛikā varṇa*) each letter is pronounced with a *bindu* which denotes Śiva

---

[32] *Ibid.*, I, 61.

[33] *Philosophical Essays*, p.168.

while *bīja* denotes Śakti. "Nāda evolves from the mutual communion between them."[34]

V

Pratyakshakaraṇa Pañchakam (Perceptible instrumental causes of acquiring the individual bodies)

The five causes of acquiring this perishable body which experiences both happiness and misery are:

1. *Karma* (physical activity, action, deed)
2. *Kāma* (longing, desire)
3. *Chandramā* (*Raja* is *Somātmaka*)
4. *Sūrya*
5. *Agni* (*Vīrya*, which is of the form of *Sūrya* and *Agni tattva*)

Of these *Sūrya, Agni* and *Chandramā* are the proximate causes of acquiring human body while *karma* and *kāma* or *vāsnā* are instrumental or *nimitta* causes, says Gorakshanātha.[35]

Karmas which are instrumental cause of creation of this body are of five kinds:

1. *Śubha karma* (good actions which bring beneficial results)
2. *Aśubha karma* (false and sinful acts resulting in evil consequences)
3. *Yaśeh* (actions which bring good name and fame and honour, such as charity etc.)
4. *Apakarsha* (actions which bring a bad name to the doer)
5. *Adṛishṭa-phala-sādhana karma* are actions whose consequences are not directly perceived by the senses.[36]

---

34 Commentary of *SSP* in *Bhāratī*, p.29; *PGN*, p.150.
35 *SSP*, I, 62.
36 *Ibid.*, I, 63.

Right or wrong, good or bad actions performed by an individual through his bodily limbs or sense organs or mental thoughts and desires are believed to exert beneficial or harmful influence upon his life, and "their psychological and moral effects greatly determine the course of his future life and even future birth". All kinds of actions, it is said, produce three kinds of effects — *dṛishṭa phala* which are visible, *adṛishṭa phala* which are "in the form of moral and religious merits and demerits (*punya-pāpa, dharma-adharma*)" which are rewarded or punished in due course of time "in accordance with the law of the cosmic order" causing happiness or misery, favourable or unfavourable conditions in this life or in the future life. The third are the *saṃskāra-phala* of our actions. Such actions produce such deep rooted *saṃskāras* in our mind that they continue even in the next embodied life also. The law of *karma*, says Banerji, "refers specially to the *adṛishṭa phala* of actions which indicate the principle of moral justice in the cosmic order".[37] Patañjali says (IV.2-4) that bad deeds "put a bar upon the manifestation of the true nature of soul while the good deeds clear up".[38]

The five attributes of *Kāma* are:

1. *Rati* (intense desire for sexual union with a woman)
2. *Preeti* (mutual attachment and love)
3. *Krīḍā* (playful acts for sexual satisfaction)
4. *Kāmanā* (longing for sexual pleasure)
5. *Āturtā* (anxiousness of sexual pleasure)[39]

Here the term *Kāma* is used in the sense of sexual instinct "which is universally present in the nature of living beings and which plays an essential part in the multiplication of living creatures in the world".

---

[37] *PGN*, pp.151-153.

[38] *Yoga-Sūtra*, IV.3; *Rāja-Yoga*, p.249.

[39] *SSP*, I,64.

The sixteen *kalās* of *Chandramā* (Moon) are also described. *Kalās* here mean different kinds of *Śaktis* or forces which emanate from *Sūrya, Chandra* and *Agni* and "perform their functions in distinctive ways for the preservation and development of the individual living bodies as well as for the maintenance of harmony and order and freshness and beauty and grandeur of the cosmic system".[40]

The sixteen *Kalās* of Chandramā are: *Ullolā* which tends to increase desire for physical pleasure. Others are *Kallolinī, Uchchalantī, Unmādinī, Taranginī, Śoshiṇī, Lampaṭā, Pravṛitti, Lahirī, Lolā, Lelihānā, Prasarantī, Pravāhā, Saumyā, Prasannatā* and *Plavantī*. Each has its special quality, and influence mind and nature of all living things. The last or the seventeenth is *Nivṛitti* which remains as such even during *pralaya* and is therefore called *Amṛita-kalā*. "The aim of the *Yogī* is to transcend the domain of all other phenomenally active 16 *kalās* and enjoy the bliss of the 17th *Amṛita-kalā* through the practice of the deepest concentration of energy".[41]

The twelve *Kalās* of *Sūrya* are: *Tāpinī, Grāsikā, Ugrā, Akuñchanī, Śoshiṇī, Prabodhinī, Smarā, Ākarshiṇī, Tushṭivardhanī, Ūrmīrekhā, Kiraṇavatī, Prabhāvatī*. The thirteenth *Kalā* of *Sūrya, Nijakalā* is self-illuminated. *Tāpinī* generates heat, *Grāsikā* dispels darkness, *Ugrā kalā* is dazzling bright, *Akuñchinī* causes contraction, *Ugrā* opens up, *Śoshiṇī* absorbs water and moisture, *Prabodhinī* causes blossoming of Lotus etc. *Ākarshiṇī* pulls water from the earth towards it, *Tushṭivardhanī* gives satisfaction to living beings, *Urmī* measures longevity, *Kiraṇavatī* spreads the rays all over and *Prabhavatī* illuminates.[42]

And the ten *Kalās* of *Agni* are: *Dīpakā, Rājikā, Jwālinī, Visphulinginī, Prachandā, Pāchikā, Raudrī, Dāhikā, Rāgiṇī,*

---

40 *Ibid.*, I,65; *PGN*, p.157.

41 *Ibid; Bhāratī*, Dec. 2004, p.30.

42 *SSP*, I.66.

Śikhāvatī. The 11th *Kalā*, which is its own transcendent *Kalā* is named *Jyoti*.

It has been pointed out that in the *Vedic* texts, *Sūrya, Agni* and *Chandra* are often glorified as Brahma and it appears that the three "have not only their individual and cosmic aspects, but also their transcendent aspects".[43]

Gorakhanātha concludes his comprehensive account of the nature of human organism by mentioning the ten principal *Nāḍīs* and their position and ten *Vāyus* (*Prāṇa*) and their location. More important of these *nāḍīs*, such as *Sushumnā, Iḍā, Pingalā*, etc., have been described in subsequent pages where they figure. Here it may be mentioned that the principal *nāḍīs* are connected with "the principal organs of perception, action and respiration". The network of these innumerable *nāḍīs*, all interlinked, are said to be always in flowing condition (*vahati*) and "carry energy from every part of the body to every other part of the body and thus unify the whole system". It has been pointed out that any attempt to verify empirically, the physiological findings of the *yogīs* by modern experimental methods would be futile because "the viewpoints, methods and purposes of the two are fundamentally different". *Yogī*'s object is to acquire perfect control over his mind and body, the entire physiological organism, including the nervous system by meditation and *yogic* discipline and he analyzes the "bodily combination" from this point of view.[44]

---

[43] *Ibid.*, I,67; *PGN*, p. 158.

[44] *Ibid.*, I,68-69; *PGN*, pp.161-162.

Chapter III

The Cosmos in the Individual Body

Gorakshanātha begins his third *Upadeśa* in his most important work, *Siddha-Siddhānta-Paddhati* (*SSP*) by saying that the *yogī* who experiences the whole cosmic system, including all the animate and inanimate existences, within the individual body is the perfect knower (*piṇḍa-jñānī*) of the body (*piṇḍa*).[1] Banerji puts it well when he says: "The complete and perfect knowledge of the individual body consists in rising above the spatial and temporal limitations of this body and identifying it with the whole universe, which is boundless in space and time. .... The complete truth of the individual body lies in or is revealed in the whole universe, — in the infinitely diversified and organised Cosmic Body of Śiva, — and the real glory of the human body ... lies in the possibility of realising the presence of this whole universe in it. The phenomenally infinite and eternal Cosmic Order is realisable in this obviously finite and transient body, the macrocosm is realisable in the microcosm. When the *yogic* vision is attained, the individual feels himself *Viśvarūpa* or *Virāṭ-Purusha* (Cosmic Personality). ...."[2]

The idea of macrocosm being realisable in the microcosm is found in many works. Thus Matsyendranātha, the Guru of Gorakshanātha, says in *Kaula-Jñāna-Nirṇaya* that there are seven nether worlds (*sapta-pātāla*) below and the seven heavens (*svarga*) above and these fourteen worlds also rest within the body in the form of *tattvas*.[3] Similarly, Sarah says

---

[1] *Siddha-siddhānta-paddhati* (*SSP*). III.1.

[2] *PGN*, p.201

[3] *Kaula-jñāna-nirṇaya* (*KJN*), Paṭala II, vss.4-5.

"Here (within the body) is the Sarasvatī, here the Gangā-sāgara (the mouth of the Gangā), here are Prayāga and Vārāṇasī, here the sun and the moon, here are the sacred places, here the *pīṭhas* and *up-pīṭhas*, I have not seen a place of pilgrimage and an abode of bliss like my body".[4]

Kshemarāja in his Commentary on the *Śiva-Sūtras* (I.14) expresses the same idea in a somewhat subtle way. He says that to a *yogī* who has accomplished identity with the Universal Consciousness, all that is perceptible inwardly or outwardly like his own body or identical with himself, "his feeling is 'I am this' (*ahmidam*), just as the feeling of Sadāśiva with regard to the entire universe is 'I am this'". To him the body appears as "an objective perceptible phenomenon ... whether that body is in the form of *deha* or the physical body (as in waking consciousness), or in the form of *dhī* or the mind (as in dream), or *prāṇa* (as in deep sleep), or as *śūnya* or mere void (as in the case of the *śūnya-pramātā*). So, in the body and in everything external, his awareness is one of undifferentiated consciousness ..."[5]

In *Jñānatilaka*, Goraksha puts the same idea in a simple understandable language when he says, "*Tūmbī men tirloka samāyā, Tirveṇī Riva Chandā*", i.e. in this body, all the three *Lokas* exist, including *Triveṇī tīrtha*, sun and moon".[6]

We thus find that the *Tantras* regarded the human body and mind, the microcosm, as "an exact parallel or counterpart of the macrocosm (external world)", and though for a different reason, the medical schools had also emphasised the same idea. Thus Charaka says that "the evolution and the nature of man resembles the evolution of the universe. All kinds of concrete existences in the universe find their exact parallels, and counterparts in the human system. Charaka further says

---

4 *Dohākośa*, p.23, Nos.96-97.

5 *Śiva-Sūtras*, I.14, p.57.

6 *Jñānatilaka* in *Gorakhabānī*, p.216.

that the causes of production, growth, decay and destruction of the universe and of man are exactly the same. .... The same law of *pariṇāma* which guides the universe guides also the evolution of man". But the Tantra went much further, continues Surendrnath Dasgupta in his *Philosophical Essays* "to establish the parallelism with elaborate details in order to help the *yogī* to narrow the field of his concentration to himself alone so that during his practice or *sādhanā*, he may find that he is a complete solar system in himself, a perfect and finished universe. This was naturally calculated to help him to concentrate his attention on himself, for when he has known himself, he has known the universe. They symbolised different parts of the body as sun, moon, stars, mountains, rivers etc., and mapped the whole body according to the world outside. But the most important point in this connection is that the creative force of the universe, which was identified with the *varṇas* or letters, was placed in diverse parts of the body".[7] The last part of Dasgupta's observation has been taken up later when dealing with the *chakras*.

The "intimate relation" between human body and cosmic spheres can be examined from another angle also. It is said that in various *yogic* traditions dating back to the Vedic period "the boundary between the symbolic and the actual — between the figurative and the literary — is blurred, so is between physiology and cosmology. Consequently, in such traditions, it is common for human attributes to be spoken of in cosmological terms, and correspondingly, for cosmic phenomenon to be discussed using anthropomorphic language". In this context, the story of the sacrifice of the Cosmic Purusha, which led to the creation of the universe from different pars of his "ostensibly enormous human body", becomes relevant.

[7] S.N. Dasgupta, *Philosophical Essays*, p.168.

"From the mind the moon was born,
From the eye the sun,
From his mouth Indra and the fire,
From his breath, the wind was born.
From his navel arose the atmosphere,
From his feet the earth, and from his ear
The cardinal points of the compass:
So did (the Gods) fashion forth these worlds".
(*Ṛ V*, 10.90.13-14, Trans. Zachner, 1966:10 cited by Mikel Burley, *Haṭha-Yoga*, p.144)

In later literature also, as we have seen, "the human being is regarded as a microcosm and, as such, he is the locus of all levels of existence and an embodied stairway to the transcendent reality. He is, in short, *kshudra-brahmāṇḍa* or little cosmos".[8]

In this context it is pertinent to note that the Tantras and Yogic works contain mainly ways or rather "key for unlocking the door to the mysteries that are hidden within the human phycho-physical complex. Also the image of the human body containing sun, moon, rivers, seas, mountains, sacred places (Prayāga, Vārāṇasī etc.), *pīṭhas*, and *up-pīṭhas* are found both in Hindu and Buddhist traditions, for example in Sarahapāda's songs.

Similarly, we find *Śiva-Saṃhitā* saying that in this body are Mount Meru, the seven continents, seers, sages, *nakshatras*, fire, water, earth, sun, moon, *pīṭha-devatas*, all the beings which exist in the three worlds. "The *yogī* alone knows all this, without doubt".[9]

In the light of the above discussion, now it would be more easy to understand the relevance of the elaborate description of the location of *Lokas*, mountains, rivers, planets etc., in the

---

[8] *Ṛig-Veda*, 10.90.13-14, Trans. Zachner, 1966; 10 cited by Mikel Burley, *Haṭha-Yoga*, p.144.

[9] *Śiva Saṃhitā*, II, vss.1-5.

human body, which otherwise would appear less meaningful to a reader who has no idea of the thought behind this important assumption.

In *Siddha-Siddhānta-Paddhati*, Gorakshanātha describes the location of the seven lower worlds, the *Lokas*, the *Devas*, the *Yakshas* etc., in the individual body. Kūrma, in the form of support of the body, is perceived as located in the *pādatala* (soles of the feet). The seven lower *lokas* (*sapta-pātāla*) are perceived in different parts of the body from toes of the feet to the thighs. These are Pātāla in the great toe of the foot, Talātala in the forepart of the great toe, Rasātala in the forepart, Sutala in region of the ankle, Vitala in the thighs, Atala in knee region. The presiding deity of these *sapta-pātāla* is Rudra. The element of anger in the *piṇḍa* is Kālāgni Rudra. He dwells in the individual body (*Vyashṭi-piṇḍa*) in the form of *krodha* (anger and wrath), says Goraksha.[10]

The three *lokas* viz., Bhū or Prithvi, Bhuvaḥ and Svaḥ are located respectively in *Guhya-sthāna*, *Liṅga-sthāna* and *Nābhi-sthāna* i.e. in the regions of *Mūlādhāra, Svādhishṭhāna* and *Maṇīpūra*. The presiding deity or governing and controlling power of these *Triloka* is Indra who is conceived as dwelling within the individual body and controlling all the powers of sense-perception (*jñānendriya*), says Goraksha.[11]

Continuing the description of the *lokas* (worlds), Gorakshanātha conceives *Mahaḥ loka* as located in the base of Merudaṇḍa, in its *Kuhara* (hole) is *Janaḥ Loka*, in the *nāla* of the column is *Tapaḥ Loka* and in *Mūlādhāra Chakra* is located the *Satyaloka*. The presiding deities of these four *lokas* are Śiva, Brahmā and other glorious Devatās (who are all self-manifestations of Śiva and Śakti). These deities are perceived as dwelling within the body, says *SSP*.[12]

---

[10] *SSP*. III.2.

[11] *Ibid.*, III.3.

[12] *Ibid.*, III.4.

Just as in the Brahmāṇḍa there are Vishṇuloka and other higher *lokas*, in the same way, in the individual body also, there are higher and lower *lokas*, which are manifestations of Śiva-Śakti, and by perceiving them, the *sādhaka* beholds the Supreme Spirit, the Paramātman. The following are the location and the presiding deities of the other *lokas* in the individual body as described in *SSP*:

Vishṇu *loka* is conceived to be located in *Kukshi* i.e. navel region, presiding deity is Vishṇu; in the heart is perceived *Rudra-loka*, its presiding deity is Rudra, ever ready to carry out destruction in his *ugra rūpa;* in the chest, a little above the heart is perceived *Īśvara-loka*, presiding deity Īśvara; in the *Kanṭha* (throat) is *Nīlakanṭha-loka*, where dwells the eternal Nīlakanṭha (Śiva). At the root of the tongue is *Bhairava loka*, the seat of Bhairava deva, says *SSP*.

In *Lalāṭa deśa* or region of the forehead is conceived *Anādi loka* where Anādi (Śiva) dwells in the centre of the *pinḍa*. A little over the eye-brows is *Kula loka* where Kuleśvara with His Śakti is seated. *Akuleśa loka* is perceived to be in the region above the *Śaṅkha nāḍī*, at *Nalini-sthāna* where dwells Akuleśvara deva (Parama Śiva); *Para- Brahma-loka* is in Brahma-randhra where *ananta* Para-Brahma is seated. In Ūrdhva-Kamala-Sahasarāra is seated the Supreme Being, Parameśvara in *parāpara bhāva*. In *Trikūṭasthāna* is *Śakti loka* where dwells Parā Śakti. In this way, twenty-one *Brahmāṇḍa-sthāna*, including *Sapta pātāla*, are perceived to be located in the individual body.[13] It has been observed that "all these *lokas* are conceived as different planes of phenomenal existences within the Cosmic Body of the Supreme Spirit. These higher *lokas* are above the regions of normal and even supernormal sense-experiences, and some of them are even above the range of our ordinary mental and intellectual conceptions. But when the individual phenomenal

[13] *Ibid.*, III.5.

consciousness is enlightened and the capacity for *yogic* experience is adequately developed through appropriate concentrated meditation in pursuance of the teachings of competent *Gurus*, the consciousness can inwardly rise to those planes and vividly experience the truth pertaining to them within the body".[14]

Just as in the Brahmāṇḍa, the seven seas and the seven *dvīpas* exist, in the same way, these are perceived as existing within the individual body.

In *majjā* (bone marrow) is Jambū dvīpa, in the bones Śaka dvīpa, in *pravāhikā nāḍīs* the Sūkshma dvīpa, in skin the Kroncha dvīpa, in skin-pores Gomaya dvīpa, in the nails Śveta dvīpa and in flesh Plaksha dvīpa have been perceived. By concentrating on them, a *yogī* can experience them. The seven seas — Kshāra, Khīra, Dadhi, Ghṛita, Madhu, Ikshu and Amṛita *samudra* are also conceived in different secretions, and fluid elements in the body.[15]

The nine *khanḍas* also exist in the individual body in the *nava-dvāras* or the nine doors of the body, says *SSP*. The *khaṇḍas* are *Bhārata khaṇḍa*, *Kāshmīr khaṇḍa*, *Karpara khaṇḍa* (in mouth), *Śrī Khaṇḍa* (in the right nostril opening), and at the opening of the left nostril *Śaṅkha khaṇḍa*, *Ekapāda khaṇḍa* in the left eye, *Gāndhāra khaṇḍa* in the right eye, *Kaivarta khaṇḍa* in the right ear aperture and in the right ear opening exists *Mahāmeru khaṇḍa*. By concentrating on these nine *Khaṇḍas*, a *Yoga sādhaka* can experience them, says *SSP*.[16]

Coming to *Ashṭa Kula Parvata* (the eight mountains), in Meru Danda or spinal column is Sumeru, in the head Kailāsh Parvata, in the back the Himālaya, in the left shoulder Malaya, Mandarāchala in the right shoulder, in the right ear is

[14] *PGN*, p.203.
[15] *SSP*. III.7-8.
[16] *Ibid.*, III.9.

Maināka, Śrī Śaila in the forehead, and in the fingers other large or small mountain ranges. By concentrating on them, says Goraksha, a *Yoga Sādhaka* can experience them within his own body.

Just as in the Brahmāṇḍa, says Goraksha, there are rivers like Gangā and others, in the principal *nāḍīs* of the individual body all the large and small rivers can be experienced. Gangā in *Iḍā nāḍī*, Yamunā in *Pingalā*, Sarasvatī in *Sushumnā*, and Pīnasā, Chandrabhāgā, Pipāsā, Śatarudrā, Śrīrātri, Narmadā are conceived as flowing in the main *nāḍīs,* and other small rivers in the remaining seventy thousand *nāḍīs*. By concentrating on these a *yoga sādhaka* can experience them in his body, says *SSP.*[17]

In our individual body are also present twenty-seven Nakshatras or constellations of stars (Aśvinī, Bharaṇī, Kṛittikā, Rohiṇī, Mṛigaśirā, Ādrā, Punarvasu, Pushya, Pūrvā-Phālgunī, Uttarā-Phālguni, Hasta, Chitrā, Swāti, Mūla, Revatī etc. Twelve Rāśis or signs of Zodiac (Mesha, *Vṛischika*, Vṛasha, Mithuna, Karka, Singh, Kanyā, Tulā, Dhanu, Makara, Kumbha, Mīna) and the nine *Grahas* (planets) (*navagraha*), viz., Sūrya, Chandra, Mangala, Budha, Guru, Śukra, Śani, Rāhu, Ketu, and also the fifteen *Tithis* (Pratipadā etc.) — all these can be located in the muscles and seventy two thousand *koshṭhas*, says Gorakshanātha.

Thirty-three crore *Devatās* dwell in countless skin pores, Dānavas, Yakshas, Rākshasas, Piśāchas, Bhūtas and Pretas in the joints of the bones, Gandharva, Kinnara, Kimpurushas, Apsarās, they all reside within the body. The *Mātra Śaktis* dwell in the force of *Vāyu*, and cloud in the tears, countless *Siddhas* in the light of the intellect, Moon in the left eye and the Sun in the right eye, planets, creepers, grasses too can be experienced by a *Yogī* within his body.[18]

---

[17] *Ibid.*, III.10-11.

[18] *Ibid.*, III.12.

Thus according to Gorakshanātha, *Viśvarūpa Parameśvara Paramātmā* resides in every individual body and a *Yogī* can behold or perceive this *Viśvarūpa* not only in his own body but in the body of every other individual and one who knows this is no doubt a *Piṇḍa-saṃvitti yogī*.[19] For him there is no essential difference between the individual and the Cosmos. It has been rightly observed that he experiences oneness with all living beings which makes him free from all hatred or fear, envy or hostility towards others, and when he looks at all things alike "what he aims at is the Brahman and in Him he rests".[20]

[19] *Ibid.*, III.13.

[20] *PGN*, pp.204-205.

Chapter IV

Inner Aspects of the Body

In the second *Upadeśa* titled *Piṇḍa-vichāra*, Gorakshanātha has discussed in *Siddha-Siddhānta-Paddhati* inner aspects of the body for those who wish to be initiated in the *Yoga* system. Matsyendra says that for introspective of meditation, understanding of the *piṇḍa* is essential.[1] The information contained in the *Upadeśa* is not based on physiological observations nor experimentation but on '*yogic* introspection and meditation'.

Nine Chakras: These are conceived as different points or stations in the *Sushumnā nāḍī* or *Brahma Mārga* (path of realisation of Brahman, the Supreme Spirit). *Sushumnā* passes through the spinal column linking *Mūlādhāra*, the lowest center of vital and psychical energy, with *Sahasarāra* which is the highest. These *chakras* influence the direction of the flow of energy and represent different planes of spiritual experience. Gorakshanātha's guru, Matsyendranātha, has also described the *chakras* in *Kaula-jñāna-nirṇaya* and *Yogavishaya.*[2]

These *chakras* and *nāḍīs* are not "physical constituents". They are, according to one view, "in the *prāṇamaya kośa*, the vital sheath in the subtle body. Only their impact is felt through the nerves ... They are seats of vital energy. They absorb and distribute *prāṇa* to the *prāṇamaya kośa* and through it to the physical body".[3] In *Yoga*, specially in the

---

1 *Kaula-Jñana-Nirṇaya* (*KJN*), *Paṭala* III.4.

2 *Ibid.*, vss.5-10; *Yogavishaya*, vs.8.

3 *Śiva-Sūtras*, Intro.lv.

Haṭha-Yoga, the concept of *chakra* or the symbolic idea of *chakra* plays a vital role. For the *yogī*, as has been rightly observed, "the 'lotus flowers' are real existing centres which are even localisable in different parts of the body".[4]

As the energy ascends higher and higher piercing the *chakras,* it reaches the highest, *Sahasrāra*, where it enjoys "the blissful experience of the identity of the individual soul with Śiva, the Supreme Spirit, as well as the eternal union of the *Mahā-Śakti* manifested in this cosmic order", as Banerji writes. It is believed that every individual has Divine Power of infinite potential but it remains dormant till awakened. The Divine Power is conceived as existing in the form of a sleeping serpent coiled round and closely embracing the lowest centre of 'physical, vital and psychical energy'. As this *Kuṇḍalinī Śakti* after being awakened rises upwards in the *Sushumnā Nāḍī*, the *sādhaka*'s vital and mental energy and his spiritual yearning become highly intense and powerful.[5] Before taking up Gorakshanātha's description of the nine *chakras* in *Siddha-Siddhānta-Paddhatī*, we may give different views about the number of *chakras*.

Matsyendranātha in *Kaula-jñāna-nirṇaya* says that there are eleven *chakras* and also the 1000 petalled one. After saying that for inner part of meditation, understanding of the *piṇḍa* is essential he says that in the *piṇḍa* are *chakras* of 4, 16, 64, 100 and 1000 petal lotuses and above it are lotus of 1,00,00,000 petals and 3,00,00,00,000 petalled lotus and above it is "all compassing, eternal, undivided lotus, pervading all and by its will it causes creation and dissolution".[6]

Some of the Hindu Tantras and texts on *Yoga* have conceived of six nerve plexuses or *shaṭ-chakra*, the Buddhist

---

4 Hinze, p.25.

5 *Philosophy of Gorakshanātha* (*PGN*), 171-72.

6 *KJN, Paṭala* V, 25-27, III.4, 5, 10-13.

have conceived three plexuses or lotuses which they identified with the three *kāyas* — the lowest *chakra* near the navel (*Maṇīpūra chakra*) representing the *Nirmāṇa-kāya*, the *chakra* near the heart is identified with *Dharma-kāya*, and the *chakra* just below the neck is said to be *Sambhoga-kāya*. The *Vajra* or *Sahaja-kāya* is located in the *Ushaṇīsha-kamala* or *Sahasrāra* of the Hindus.[7] Gorakshanātha has described nine *chakras*. The number of *chakras* is said to be even more than nine. Thus between *Svādhishṭhāna chakra* and *Maṇīpūra chakra* (in the navel region) there are said to be three distinct centres and there are believed to be six *chakras* beyond the *Sahasrāra*.[8] However, some authors consider six *chakras* as the most important ones. Hinze in his analytical study regards *Mulādhāra* (in the region between the genitals and anus), *Svādhishṭhāna* (a little over the genitals), *Anāhat chakra* (in the region of the heart), *Viśuddha chakra* (in the region of the larynx), *Ajñā chakra* (between the eye-brows) and *Sahasrāra* (in the top of the head) as the most important ones. Every *chakra*, he writes, is symbolically represented as a lotus with fixed number of petals.[9] Later, we will take up his analysis of the sequential series of the *chakras*, number of their petals and their connection with the five classical elements.

John Woodroffe calls the six *chakras* as vital centres within the spinal column. "They are centres of *Prāṇa Śakti* manifested by *Prāṇa-vāyu* in the living body ... not perceptible to the gross senses".[10]

The nine *chakras* mentioned by Gorakshanātha in *Siddha-Siddhānta-Paddhati* may now be described at some length.

---

[7] *Obscure Religious Cults*, p.91.

[8] *Siddha-Siddhānta-Paddhati* (*SSP*), II, vs.1; Gopinath Kaviraj's paper, Chakras according to Gorakhanātha, Saraswati Bhavan Series, Vol.II, 1923.

[9] Hinze, p.31,

[10] J. Woodroffe, *Śakti and Śākta* (*JWSS*), p.435.

The first of the nine *chakras* within the *pinḍa* is *Brahma chakra* or *Mulādhāra chakra* (in the region between the genitals and anus). It is conceived as conical with three coils. The three coils have been interpreted as representing the three *guṇas* of Śakti viz. *Sattva, Rajas* and *Tamas* but She "transcends the three *guṇas*, since in its essential nature She is identical with Śiva". Near the *Brahma chakra* is *Mūlakanda* where, *SSP* says, the *Yogī* should meditate on Śakti in the form of fire. There is also *Kāmarūpa pīṭha*. By meditating here, says Goraksha, all desires are fulfilled. Pūrṇānandayati says in *Śri-tattva-chintāmaṇi* that the *Ādhāra-chakra* has four petals on which are written Va, Śa, Sha, and Sa.[11]

The second is *Svādhishṭhāna chakra*. In this *chakra* is said to be a Śivaliṅga of red colour, facing in the opposite direction which should be meditated upon, says Goraksha. Here is also the *Uḍḍiyāna-pīṭha*. To raise his psycho-vital energy to this plane (*Svādhishṭhāna chakra*) the *Yogī* or the *sādhaka* should meditate upon the Śivaliṅga. *Śrī-tattva-chintāmaṇi* says that contemplation on the *Svādhishṭhāna Lotus* destroys *kāma* (lust), *krodha* (anger), *lobha* (greed), *moha* (delusion), *mada* (pride), *matsaryya* (envy), which arise from *Ahaṃkāra*, and the sun of knowledge (*Jñāna*) is acquired.[12]

The third is *Nābhi-chakra* (also called *Maṇīpūra chakra*) in the region of the navel resembling a coiled serpent, and within the *chakra*, *Kuṇḍalinī Śakti* reveals Herself with the brilliance of millions of morning Suns. By meditation upon Her, all the *siddhis* or supernatural powers are attained, says *SSP*. The *Kuṇḍalinī Śakti* in *Nābhi chakra* or *Maṇīpūraka chakra* has been called *Madhya Śakti* "indicating that this is also the intermediate stage of the self-revelation of the essential character of Śiva-Śakti".[13]

---

[11] *SSP*, II.1, *Shaṭ-Chakra-Nirūpaṇa*, pp.330-31 in *The Six Centres and the Serpent Power* (*SCSP*); *PGN*, pp.173-174.

[12] *SSP*, II.2; *Shaṭ-Chakra-Nirūpaṇa*,(*SCN*), v.18, p.364 in *SCSP*.

[13] *Ibid.*, II.3; *PGN*, p.177.

The fourth *chakra*, called *Hṛidaya-chakra* or *Anāhata-chakra* is located near the heart in the *Sushumnā Nāḍī*. It is described as eight petalled lotus facing downwards. It is known as *anāhata* because it is here that the sound of *Śabda Brahman* is heard. *SSP* says that one should meditate on the steady light (*jyoti*) of the form of Śiva*liṅga* in the middle of the *karṇikā* of the lotus. This Śakti is called *Haṃsa-kalā*. By doing so all the sense-organs of the *sādhaka* come under his control, says *SSP*. In that state, his mind is freed from all desires and egoistic feelings and he becomes 'an embodiment of calmness and tranquility even in the normal state of existence'.[14]

The fifth is *Kaṇṭha-chakra*, also known as *Viśuddha-chakra* in the region of the larynx. Here on the left is *Iḍā* or *Chandra-Nāḍī* and on the right *Pingalā* or *Sūrya-Nāḍī* and between these two is *Sushumnā* (*Brahma-Nāḍī*). One should meditate upon *Sushumnā*, which is also called *Anāhata Kalā*. By mediating upon it, says *SSP*, the *sādhaka* is blessed with *Anāhata Siddhi* as a result of which all determinations and desires of his mind are fulfilled.[15]

The sixth is *Tālu-chakra* located at the root of the palate. Here, there is continuous flow of ambrosia or *amṛita* from *Chandra-manḍala* situated in *Sahasradala*. In *tālu-mūla* there is a *ghanṭikā* of the shape of *liṅga*. From its base there is a hole till the end of the palate called *Rājadanta*. This is called *Śaṅkhinī vivara*. This is connected with Śaṅkhinī Nāḍī. This is also the way of the *Daśama-dwāra* (tenth door). Here, says *SSP*, the *yogī* should meditate on *Śūnya* (*Nirguṇa Nirākāra Alakha Nirañjana Parameśvara*). By doing so, one attains the state of *chitta-laya* or dissolution of individual consciousness in the Universal Consciousness.[16]

---

[14] *Ibid.*, II.4; *PGN*, p.177.

[15] *Ibid.*, II.5; Cf. *PGN*, p.178.

[16] *Ibid.*, II.6; *PGN*, p.179.

The seventh is *Bhrū-chakra*. It is also called *Ājñā-chakra* as well as *Muktitriveṇī*. It is located at the nerve-centre between the eye-brows. At the centre of the *Bhrū-chakra* is the *Jñāna-netra* of the shape of the flame of a lamp. By meditating on it, one becomes *Vāk-siddha*. Pūrṇānanda Yati says that the *Ājñā* lotus has two petals with letters Ha and Ksha. According to *Gautamīya Tantra*, it is here that the *Ājñā* of the Gurū is communicated. Here within the triangle in this *chakra*, says *Śri-tattva-chintāmaṇi,* "dwells the combination of letters which form the *Praṇava*".[17]

The eighth is *Nirvāṇa-chakra*, also called *Brahma-randhra*. It is like the shape of the tip of a needle and of the size of *dhūma-śikhā*. A *Yogī* should meditate on it, says *SSP*. This is also the *Jālandhara Pīṭha*, the bestower of *moksha.*[18] It is here that the individual consciousness is merged in the Universal Consciousness and *Kuṇḍalinī Śakti* is united with Śiva.

The ninth is *Akāśa-chakra* (located at the highest point of *Sahasrāra* and above the *Nirvāṇa-chakra* in the *Brahma-randhra)*. It is described by *SSP* as a lotus of sixteen petals facing upwards. In the *karṇikā* of the lotus is *Śakti* facing upwards and it is of the form of a *trikūṭa*. This is *Parama-śūnya*, which should be meditated on. This is also the *Pūrṇagiri-pīṭha* which fulfils all the desires.[19]

We note that Gorakshanātha lays great emphasis on contemplation on these *chakras* as by doing so various benefits and *siddhis* would come to the *sādhaka* and one could even attain *moksha*. The multiple benefits and various powers which come as a result of "collective meditation" on these *chakras* have also been described by Goraksha's guru Matsyendranātha in *Kaula-jñāna-nirṇaya*.[20] As has been

---

[17] *Ibid.*, II.7; *Rudra-yāmala*, ch.XXVII, vs.68; *SCN*, vss.32, 35 in *SCSP*, pp.394-95, 402-403.

[18] *Ibid.*, II.8.

[19] *Ibid.*, II.9.

[20] *KJN, Paṭala*, XIV.

explained later, the *varṇas* or letters on the petals of the *chakras* are identified with the creative force of *Mātṛikā* of the universe and different *chakras* are regarded as "seats of different forces of the *Mātṛikā-Śakti*". As the *sādhaka* identifies himself with each of these *chakras* (centres of different forces) during the ascent of the *Kuṇḍalinī Śakti* to *Sahasrāra* the influence of these forces binding him ceases as he passes from one centre of force to another until he identifies himself with the Supreme Spirit and is liberated.

As the *chakras* have a special place in the *Kuṇḍalinī-Yoga*, their nature and various other aspects deserve a closer study.

Hinze has tried to draw useful conclusions from the sequential series of the *chakras*, number of their petals and their connection with the five classical Elements, taking into account the *Yantras* also representing the lotuses. He has explained these through the following table[21]:

No.	*Chakra*	Number of Petals	Illustrations
7	Sahasrāra	1000 petals	
6	Ājñā	2 petals	6
5	Viśuddha	16 petals	5
4	Anāhata	12 petals	4
3	Maṇipūra	10 petals	3
2	Svādhisṭhāna	6 petals	2
1	Mūlādhāra	4 petals	1

One reason for different number of petals each *chakra* has (4 in *Mūlādhāra*, 6 in *Svādhishṭhāna* etc.) is said to be that "the number of petals in any *chakra* is determined by the number and position of the *Nāḍīs* or Yoga "nerves" around the *chakra*. Thus, 4 *Nāḍīs* surrounding and passing through the vital movements of the *Mūlādhāra chakra* give it the appearance of a lotus of four petals. The petals are thus

[21] Hinze, p.31.

configuration made by the position of the *nāḍīs* at any particular centre". These *nāḍīs* are not "gross physical nerves" known to a Vaidya of *Āyurveda* but "subtle channels (*Vivara*) along which the *Prāṇik* currents flow", like ocean currents, which to a superficial eye may look similar but when closely examined they will be found moving with "varying degrees of force in all directions".[22]

With the first five lotus flowers are connected, says Hinze, 'the five classical "Elements" which are signified by definite geometrical figures (*yantras*)' as shown below:

Lotus	Element	Yantra's shape
16 petals (Viśuddha)	*ākāśa* (ether)	Circle
12 petals (Anāhata)	*vāyu* (air)	Hexagram
10 petals (Maṇīpūra)	*tejas* (fire)	Triangle (with *Swāstika* forms)
6 petals (Svādhishṭhāna)	*apaḥ* (water)	Waxing crescent moon
4 petals (Mūlādhāra)	*pṛithvī* (earth)	Square

He further points out that each of the five elements is characterized by a Central Sound or seed sound (*Bīja-mantra*) visible in the form of a Devanāgirī letter in the middle of the lotus.[23] Matsyendranātha in *Kaula-jñāna-nirṇaya* has described 7 categories of *Bīja*-mantra, the initial letters of different series of mantras being ksha, la, ha, sa, sha, śa, va, hla. Of these, he says, 'ksha' is in the Brahmarandhra, 'la' in the forehead, 'ha' between the eyebrows, 'sa' in the mouth, 'sha' in the *kaṇṭha*, 'śa' in the heart, 'va' in the navel and 'hla' in the Mūlādhāra (X.vss.6-8).[24] The petals of the lotus have Devanāgirī letters which Hinze calls 'peripheral sound'. Also above every letter there is a *bindu* suggesting nasal

---

[22] J. Woodroffe, *Śakti and Śākta* (*JWSS*), p.436.
[23] Hinze, p.32.
[24] *KJN*, X, vss.6-8.

pronunciation and showing that the letters have a 'sacred aim in this context'.

The total number of petals of the first six lotus flowers comes to 50, the usual number of letters of the (cultic) Devanāgarī, leaving *kśhakāra* (for its reason, see Hinze, p.35 and n.36 and 55ff). "This alphabet is contained twenty-times in the 1000 petalled lotus. The Sahasrāra lotus thus is the potentiated sum of the lower lotus-flowers", he writes.

The six lotuses (*Mūlādhāra, Svādhishṭhāna* etc.) should be considered "as the main stages of the (*Kuṇḍalinī*) *Śakti* on her way from the heaven (microcosmically: thc region of the head, the 2-and 1000 petalled lotus the region of pure, undimmed consciousness and is thus the realm of Śiva and home of Śakti") to earth (microcosmically: the 4 petalled lotus (*Mūlādhāra*)".

Now Śakti is the creator of the five elements from the finest *Ākāśa*, to the grossest *Pṛithvī*, a process of "gradual condensation of the primordial substance (*Prakṛiti*). When the earth element is created, the Śakti is completely exhausted and She "lies rolled together and sleeps in the four petalled lotus. This aspect of Śakti is Kuṇḍalinī", he says.

"The emigration of Śakti out of her spiritual home into the earthy region of gross matter" also brings with it gradual, step by step, "veiling of the pri-mordial consciousness". To overcome this illusion and to reincorporate his personal consciousness with the Universal Consciousness as he tries to wake up the 'sleeping' *Kuṇḍalinī Śakti*, so that she again goes up to her proper home, the 1000 petalled lotus.

On its way towards the *Sahasrāra*, the awakened Śakti re-absorbs all that she had created during her earlier descent, the elements, the seed-sounds, the sense-qualities and everything in the respective lotuses, until she reaches the 1000 petalled lotus to unite with the Universal Consciousness, when the *Yogī* experiences the highest ecstasy (*samādhi*).

Normally a *Yogī* cannot remain in *samādhi* for a long time as "a natural impulse leads the *Kuṇḍalinī Śakti* again, step by step below so that little by little the reabsorbed worlds are newly created". The process of dissolution and recreation of the microcosmic world, goes on. "The 'dissolution' of the microcosmic world experienced by the *Yogī* is a 'dissolution' as seen from one side only; juxtaposed against it, there is a 'coming into Being' in the spiritual world", writes Hinze.[25]

The above account does help us in understanding the importance of the *chakras* in the body. (for parallelisms to the symbolism of the seven lotus-flowers in other traditions — *Saundaryalahirī*, the cult of Mithra, the Gnosis and Western Mysticism, refer Hinze, pp.38ff).

We have noted that Gorakshanātha in his description of the *chakras* repeatedly asks to concentrate on the *chakras* (he does so in case of *Ādhāras, Lakshyas* and *Vyoma* also, as we will presently see). The idea of concentration is based on the ground that in *Yoga* "we find that the mind, when concentrated on any *tattva* in such a way that the *yogin* becomes one with that, naturally passes through its inner dynamic or *rajas* into the subtler and subtler *tattvas* until it goes to *buddhi* and is finally liberated, for here the *yogin* perceives that he is pure *purusha* and is essentially different from *prakṛiti*".[26]

Now in Tantra, *Yoga* is defined as "the union of the *Jivātma* and Paramātmā or Parama Śiva". We have noted that petals of all the *chakras* have *varṇas* or letters are identified with the creative force of the universe, called *Mātṛikā*. Her self was formed of the fifty letters from '*a*' to '*ha*', and different *chakras* are regarded as "seats of the different forces of the *Mātṛikā-śakti* and are associated with diverse passions etc."

In the doctrine of *Shaṭ-chakra-bheda* "the *jīva* in the

---

[25] Hinze, pp.32-38.

[26] *Philosophical Essays*, p.174.

Kuṇḍalinī is roused up and as it gradually identifies itself with different *chakras*, it gradually passes on and on to the *Sahasrāra,* .... the different *chakras* are seats of the different forces of the *Mātṛīkā-Śakti* and are associated with diverse passions etc.

"Now as the *sādhaka* identifies with each of these centres of force (*chakras*) the influence of these forces in binding him ceases and as he passes from one centre of force to another until he identifies himself with the *Paramātman* and is liberated."[27]

We thus find that there are more than one way of understanding the *chakras*.

Why so much emphasis or meditation on the *varṇas* on the petals of the chakras? As S.N. Dasgupta says, in the Tantras, great importance is attached to *śabda* or sound. In fact from the very beginning of philosophic speculation, *śabda* or sound was regarded as eternal. The Tantras assume that "the movement which has produced the world is represented in us in miniature in the production of sound" and this process "which underlies the cosmic creation manifests itself in us in every case of the production of sound, so that the genesis of sound ... is a real symbol of the creative process". As the *varṇas* are of the nature of Parama-Śiva or Śiva-Śaktimaya, the creative force of the universe, by concentrating mind on them in such a way as to unify the *sādhaka* with the Supreme force, union of *Jivātmā* and *Paramātmā* is effected thus fulfilling the main aim of *yoga*.[28]

After describing the nine *chakras* and the object of meditating on them, Gorakshanātha gives a comprehensive description of the sixteen *Ādhāras*, three kinds of *Lakshyas* and five *Vyomas,* to help a *sādhaka* in his effort to concentrate by fixing mind at certain places or points inside or outside the

---

[27] *Ibid.*, pp.174-75.

[28] *Ibid.*, p.172-174.

body, or on *prāṇa* or *nāda*. By fixing the mind in this manner, the *vikalpas* of the mind begin to dissolve and one is absorbed in the *ātma svarūpa* or essential Self, the object being the same as that of *sthāna-kalpanā* in the Kashmir Śaivism. Gorakshanātha has given a long list of *Ādhāras, Lakshyas* and *Vyomas* giving an aspirant many options from which to choose such objects for his concentration which he finds more suitable or helpful to him in *dhyāna* or meditation leading ultimately to *samādhi*, the culmination of all efforts to control mind's *vṛittis* and *prāṇa vāyu*. The number of *Ādhāras, Lkshya* and *Vyoma* may appear unnecessarily large to a casual reader but in reality, being based on self-experience of the Mahā Yogī, they are a helpful guide in meditation leading to the dissolution of the *vikalpas* which is one of the primary objects of *Yoga*.

Sixteen Adharas:

1. The first of the sixteen *Ādhāras* or loci of concentration is *Padagushṭhādhāra* "the seat of the vital functions in each of the big toes". *SSP* says that one should concentrate on a luminous form at the fore part. This steadies the sight.[29]

2. The second is *Mūlādhāra*, "the primary seat of *Kuṇḍalinī Śakti* and the starting point of *Sushumnā Nāḍī*. It is at this *ādhāra* that the psycho-vital energy should be first concentrated and then pushed upward in the path of *Sushumnā*". The *SSP* says that the practitioner should press the *Mūlādhāra-sūtra* with the ankle of his left foot sitting in *Padmāsana*. This increases *teja* (glow) of the body and kindles the fire which dwells within.[30]

3. The third is *Gudādhāra* in the rectum. By expansion and contraction (*vikāsa-saṃkochana*) of *Gudādhāra*, the *Apāna-vāyu* is steadied. This helps in the union of *Prāna vāyu* and *Apāna vāyu*.[31]

---

[29] *SSP*, II.10,

[30] *Ibid.*, II.11; *PGN*, p.182,

[31] *SSP*, II.12,

4. The fourth is *Medhrādhāra* at the root of the sex organ. *Prāṇa-śakti*, which principally lies in *bindu* or *vīrya* or *retas* is conserved here, and the *sādhaka* is expected to be careful against losing it by keeping in control lustful propensities. *SSP* says that by shrinking the sexual organ (*liṅga-saṃkochana*), the *bindu* is made to move upwards and transcending Brahmā, Vishṇu, Rudra *granthis*, *vīrya* is made immovable, its movement arrested in *Bhramara gufā* at the upper most part of the spinal column and in the lower region of *Sahasrāra*. This is *Vajrolī kriyā* as a result of which a *yogī* is established in *akhaṇḍa brahmacharya*, his *praṇa, mana* and *vīrya bindu* are in mutual harmony and he is established in *Paramapada*.[32]

5. The fifth is *Uḍḍiyāna-ādhāra*, located in the centre between *Liṅgamūla* and *Nābhimūla*. By controlling it, quantity of faeces and urine is reduced and intestines and urinary organs are kept in order.[33]

6. The sixth is *Nābhi-ādhāra*, located at the root of *nābhi* or navel, the seat of *Nābhi-chakra*. *SSP* says that here the *nāda-laya* is manifested. This occurs when mind is merged in *nāda,* which "in its ultimate essence" is *Akshara* or *Śabda-Brahman*.[34]

7. The seventh is *Hṛidaya-ādhāra*, the seat of *Anāhat-chakra*. Here, by restraining the *Prāṇa-vāyu*, the eight petalled lotus blossoms. It is believed to be the centre of the union between *Prāṇa* and *Apāna* and it is here that the *Anāhata-Nāda* is most distinctly perceived by concentrating the mind on it. As a result of concentration of *Prāṇa* at this centre, the petals of the lotus are opened upwards. "This implies that the psycho-vital energy is not then dragged downwards or world-ward, but spontaneously moves upward in the spiritual path for self fulfilment in the higher planes.

---

[32] *Ibid.*, II.13.

[33] *Ibid.*, II.14.

[34] *Ibid.*, II.15; *PGN*, pp.184-85.

A *yogī* is, thereafter, blessed with an enlightened spiritual outlook".[35]

8. The eighth is *Kaṅṭha-ādhāra*, the seat of *Viśuddha-chakra*. By practicing *Jālandhara bandha* in which *kaṅṭha* (throat) is restrained or contracted by placing the chin on the chest, the movement of *Prāṇa vāyu* in *Iḍā* and *Piṅgalā* is controlled and the psycho-vital energy moves up in the *Sushumnā*.[36]

9. The ninth is *Ghaṅṭikā-ādhāra*, located at the root of the soft palate. By turning the tongue upward and touching the base of the *Ghanṭikā-ādhāra*, one tastes the *Amṛita-kalā* which flows from the *Chandra manḍala* in *Sahasrāra lotus*. Normally, it is not perceptible and flows down through *Iḍā* and *Pingalā* and thus wasted, but when partaken, it "attracts his attention inward for the enjoyment of spiritual bliss". This enables a *Yogī* to remain healthy and free from diseases, says *SSP*.[37]

10. The tenth, *Tālu-ādhāra*, is in a still deeper part of the palate. The *sādhaka* has to draw out and lengthen his tongue by *chālana-dohana kriyā* and then turning it backward, the tip of the tongue is made to enter the small hole within the soft root of the palate and then gently led into the innermost aperature. This helps in perfecting *Khecharī Mudrā* as a result of which the *sādhaka* becomes *niśchala* or immovable like wood. This state is called *Jaḍa-samādhi*. The great importance of *Khecharī Mudrā* and its resulting benefits are emphasissed in all works on *Yoga*.[38]

11. The eleventh is *Jihvādhāra*. It is located at the root of the tongue and the *sādhaka* by resting the tip of the tongue at this point, is freed from all the diseases.[39]

---

35 *SSP*, II.16; *PGN*, p.185.
36 *SSP*, II.17,
37 *SSP*, II.18,
38 *Ibid.*, II.19; *PGN*, p.186-187.
39 *SSP*, II.20,

12. The twelfth is *Bhrū-madhyādhāra* located at the centre of the space between the eye-brows, the seat of the *Ājñā-chakra* or *Bhrū-chakra*. By meditating on the *Chandra-maṇḍala* "the luminous disc of the moon emitting pure white and cool and tranquil rays", the practitioner's mind and body become tranquil. The practice is believed to be helpful in "steadying the attention and cooling down all types of excitements in the body and in the mind".[40]

13. The thirteenth is the *Nāsādhāra*. The *SSP* advises the *sādhaka* to fix his gaze on the tip of the nose and concentrate his attention on this point. By doing it regularly, the mind becomes stable i.e. free from restlessness and all types of excitements.[41]

14. The fourteenth is *Kapāṭādhāra*, located at the root of the nose. By concentrating mind on this point for a period of six months, says *SSP*, one beholds *jyoti-puñja*, a mass of self illumined light, which illuminates the mind.[42]

15. The fifteenth is *Lalāṭādhāra*, located at the centre of the fore-head. By meditating on the *jyoti-puñja* here, one becomes bright and virile.[43]

16. The sixteenth is *Brahma-randhra-ādhāra*. This is the place of *Ākāśa-chakra*. Here, says *SSP*, the *sādhaka* meditates on the lotus-feet of perfectly realised Śrī Guru and by his grace becomes *vyāpaka* like the *Ākāśa*. As has been pointed out, by *vyāpaka* here means that he realises the Supreme Spirit or Paramātman everywhere, within his own body as well as in the Cosmic order. Gorakshanātha has described *Ākāśa-chakra* as "*Pūrṇa-giri-pīṭha* or the realm of the most perfect spiritual-fulfilment, and has instructed the *yogī* to be absorbed in the meditation of *Parama Śūnya* i.e. the Absolute

[40] *SSP*, II.21; *PGN*, p.187.
[41] *SSP*, II.22,
[42] *Ibid.*, II.23.
[43] *Ibid.*, II.24.

Differenceless Changeless One — the unity of Śiva and Śakti and *sādhaka*".[44]

Three Lakshyas:

These are the ways to make the mind stable by concentrating on certain objects. From the point of view of *yogic* discipline, control of mind is very important.

Gorakshanātha mentions three (kinds of) *lakshyas* (*Laksha-traya*), those inside the body, some outside the body and some without any special reference to the body. On the basis of location of these objects of meditation, the *lakshyas* are of three kinds viz., *Antar-lakshya, Bahir-lakshya* and *Madhya-lakshya*.

Antar-lakshya: An aspirant is to meditate on *Kuṇḍalinī Śakti* rising upwards in *Sushumnā Nāḍī* which runs in the *Merudaṇḍa* from *Mūlakanda* (from where all the *nāḍīs* originate) to *Sahasrāra*. *Kuṇḍalinī Śakti*, says *SSP*, in luminosity and brightness, is like crores of lightenings. The *Mahāśakti Kuṇḍalinī*, on being meditated upon bestows all the *siddhis* on the *yogī*.

There are other centres of concentration within the body, which all come in the category of *Antara-lakshya* for introspective meditation. One is *Gollaṭa-maṇḍapa*, just above the forehead in the front part of the *Sahasrāra*. The aspirant should concentrate on it.

The second *Antara-lakshya* is in the *Bhramara guhā*. "Life-power is to be imagined as existing at this centre in the form of a red-coloured bee and attention is to be fixed upon it".[45] *Bhramara-guhā*, according to one view is above the spinal column in the back-part of *Sahasrāra*, above the neck.

Another *Antara-lakshya* for concentration of mind is *nāda* which is heard as '*dhūn-dhūn*' within the head when both the

[44] *SSP*, II.25; *PGN*, p.188.

[45] *SSP*, II.26-27; *PGN*, p.190.

ears are firmly closed by the fore-fingers. The *sādhaka* is advised to fix his attention upon this internal sound. On concentration, there will be realisation of the Supreme Spirit in the *nāda* which is "pure self-revelation of Śiva-Śakti in Sound form". *Nāda* is subtle in the *Madhyamā* stage and is no longer audible at the *Paśyantī* stage. "All the *vikalpas* are now calmed and one can experience the Supreme I-consciousness".

The fourth *Antara-lakshya* advised by Gorakshanātha is the form of the apple of the eye at the centre of the eyes emanating blue light. It has been observed that "deep concentration of the whole consciousness upon this *jyoti* would gradually lead to the spiritual, illumination of the consciousness and spiritualisation of his being".[46]

Bahir-lakshya: A number of external *lakshyas* have been suggested in *SSP* for concentrating thought and perception. A *sādhaka* may concentrate his attention on the presence of a bright red light at a distance of two fingers from the tip of his nose, or he may meditate on a white sheet of water with waves, ten fingers from his nose, or he may imagine *Pṛithvī-tattva* of yellow colour at a distance of twelve fingers from his nose and concentrate on it, or he may look at the sky and meditate upon it; it makes the *chitta* as pure, clear, all pervasive and giver of *mukti* as the sky itself, or the *sādhaka* may see inwardly the expanse of land of the colour of heated gold which will make his sight steady, says *SSP*.[47]

Madhya-lakshya: In this, mind or vision is not concentrated on any particular object or place. The *SSP* advises the following *Madhya-lakshyas* on which mind may be concentrated. Any object of white, red or black colour, or objects of the shape of flame of fire, or of the form of *jyoti*, or of the form of lightning, or of the form of *ardha-chandra*

---

[46] *SSP*, II.27; *PGN*, p.191.

[47] *SSP*, II.28.

(crescent Moon), or of the form of Sūryamaṇḍala, or on any full part of one's body, without imagining any particular place or spot.[48] On any of these, of his choice, the *sādhaka* has to concentrate his mind, forgetting everything else about him, to increase his power of concentration and raise his mind to higher and higher planes of spiritual experience.

Five Vyomas: Gorakshanātha, says that an adept, by meditating upon the five spaces becomes as pure, all comprehending, and full of *teja*, as the sky. Though *Vyoma* or *Ākāśa* is one, it has been conceived in five different ways to facilitate concentration of mind. These are *Ākāśa, Parākāśa, Mahākāśa, Tattvākāśa* and *Sūryākāśa*, which together are called *Vyoma-Pañchaka*. *Ākāśa* is conceived as extremely pure and formless (*nirākāra*) "empty spaces pervading and unifying the outer and the inner worlds", while *Parākāśa* is conceived as absolute darkness within and outside the body, free from all diversities, which is to be meditated upon, and *Mahākāśa* is described as the fiery space during *Pralaya* within the body which is to be meditated upon. *Tattvākāśa* is to be meditated as *nija-tattva-svarūpa* inside and outside the body, and *Sūryākāśa* is to be conceived as shining with the brilliance of crores of Sun. By meditating on these five *Vyomas*, the *sādhaka* becomes as pure, comprehending and endowed with *teja* as the *Ākāśa,* says Goraksha.[49]

Concluding the above description, Gorakshnātha says that a *Yogī* who does not know well the nine *chakras*, sixteen *ādhāras*, three *lakshyas* and the five *vyomas* located within his body is a *Yogī* in name only and does not know the principles and elements of *Yoga*.

---

[48] *Ibid.*, II.29.

[49] *Ibid.*, II.30; *PGN*, pp.193-194.

Chapter V

Ashṭāṅga-Yoga

In the *Siddha-Siddhānta-Paddhati* (*SSP*), Gorakshanātha dwells upon the *Ashṭāṅga-yoga* rather briefly. The eight *aṅga* or limbs of *Yoga* are, he says, *Yama, Niyama, Āsana, Prāṇāyāma, Pratyāhāra, Dhāraṇā, Dhyāna* and *Samādhi.*[1] Of these, the first five *aṅgas* are indirectly helpful in the *yoga-sādhanā* because they expel such tendencies which come in the way of attaining *samādhi*. These five (*Yama, Niyama, Āsana, Prāṇāyāma* and *Prathyāhāra*) are regarded as external *aṅgas* or *bahiraṅga sādhana* of *Yoga*. *Dhārṇā, Dhyāna* and *Samādhi* are the *antaraṅga* (proximate or essential) *sādhana* (means).

By *Yama*, says SSP, is meant *upaśama* i.e. to gain peace by controlling the senses. A *sādhaka* should gradually bring under control all his senses by turning them away from their respective objects of attraction and make them concentrate on the true nature of Self, and by regulating or controlling food, sleep, cold, *vāta* (windy humour of the body), and afflictions, to be prepared for the *yoga sādhanā*.[2]

Niyama, according to the *SSP*, is control of mental propensities. The signs of *Niyama* are to remain contented in all conditions, whether in loneliness or as an object of apathy of others, and to be free from attachment or envy, and to feel secure and without fear under the care of the Guru.[3]

We note that *Yama* and *Niyama* have been touched too briefly and in a very general way by Yogirāja Gorakshanātha.

---

[1] *Siddha-Siddhānta-Paddhati* (*SSP*), II.32.

[2] *Ibid.*

[3] *Ibid.*, II.33.

It may also be mentioned that in many works there is only mention of six *aṇgas* of *Yoga*, and *Yama* and *Niyama* apparently have been left out, such as in *Goraksha-Saṃhitā*, *Gorksha-Śataka*, *Maitrāyiṇī-Upanishad*, *Dhyānabindu-Upanishad*, *Manusṃriti*, *Skanda-Purāṇa* etc. The reason as Prof. P.V. Kane suggests, is that it was expected from all knowing people that they would follow *Yama* and not merely the *Niyama*.[4] *Yoga-Sūtra* of Patañjali mentions these five *Yamas*: *ahiṃsā* (non-killing), *satya* (truthfulness), *asteya* (not to accept anything which go against the *Śāstras*), *brahmacharya* (continence) and *aparigraha* (non-receiving or gathering).[5] As Manu says, every one should observe these *Yamas*. The observance of *Yama* and *Niyama* have been described as the first step towards the attainment of *mukti* or *Kaivalya* for which the *ātmā* should be cleansed of sensual and egoistic desires, Gorakshanātha's brevity on *Yama*, thus becomes understandable, for every Indian was expected to be acquainted with these principles. That is why *Amarakośa* describes these as '*nitya karma*' i.e. which are to be observed continuously. Patañjali says (II.1) that their practice — non-killing, truthfulness, chastity, etc., are to be followed by everyone, "unbroken by time, place, purpose and caste rules". They are universal great vows to be observed by every one irrespective of nation, country or position. With the establishing of non-killing, all enmities cease, by establishment of continence energy is gained, by the establishment of truthfulness, the *yogī* gets power of attaining whatever he says for the good of others.[6]

---

[4] M.M. P.V. Kane, *History of Dharma Śāstra*(*HDS*), tr. A.C. Kāsyapa, Vol.V, 270.

[5] Patañjali, *Yoga-Sūtra*, II.30-31.

[6] *HDS*, V. p.270; *Yoga-Śūtra*, II.31, 35, 38; *Rāja-Yoga*, pp.208-210. The *Smṛitis* (such as Manu, Yājñavalkya) permit their non-observance under certain conditions.

As noted, about *Niyama* also, Goraksha does not specifically mention each one of them and says that it is control or regulation of *mano-vṛittis* or mental modifications and its *lakshaṇa* is detachment, solitude, contentment and to feel happy and secure under the guru's care.[7] The five *Niyama* are *śaucha* (internal i.e. mental and external purification), *santosha* (contentment), *tapa* (mortification), *svādhyāya* (study) and *Īśvara Praṇidhāna* (devotion to God and to dedicate all actions to Him). Of these, the last three come in the category of *Kriyā yoga*. Internal purification is brought about by inculcating the virtues of *maitri* (friendliness) *karuṇā* (mercy), and *muditā* (cheerfulness). Contentment leads to happiness, *tapa* brings power to the organs of the body, and results in purification of the *sattva*, cheerfulness of mind, greater concentration, control over the *indriyās* or organs, fitness for realisation of the Supreme Spirit, and by resignation to Īśvara comes *samādhi*.[8]

Coming next to ***Āsana***, Gorakshanātha says that *Āsana* is to establish oneself in I-consciousness and the *lakshaṇa* of *Āsana* is establishment of oneself in the object of meditation sitting in any of these *āsanas*: *Swāstika āsana, Padmāsana* and *Siddhāsana*.[9] Patañjali is even more brief. He simply says "*Āsana* is that which is firm and pleasant" (I.46) but in the next *sūtra* (I.47) tells how *āsana* can be firm and pleasant. It is accomplished by abating our natural tendencies and by meditating on the Infinite, the unlimited. It results in what is called "going beyond the idea of concrete body or loosing all sense of body". The body posture having been conquered and made immune to distractions, one can proceed with the control of *prāṇa*.[10] According to Goraksha-śataka,

---

[7] *SSP*, II.33.

[8] *Yoga-Sūtra*, II.32, 33-45.

[9] *SSP*, II.34.

[10] *Yoga-Sūtra*, II.46-48.

Siddhāsana is the opener of the door of release and *Haṭha-Yoga-Pradīpikā* says that *Siddhāsana* and *Matsyāsana* awaken Kuṇḍalinī to make her ascend to the *Sahasrāra* piercing the *chakras*.[11]

As has been pointed out, *Āsana* has more importance in *yoga* than in *sādhanā*. The principle as regard *Āsana* is "to secure a comfortable seat, because that is favourable to meditation and worship generally. If one is not comfortable, there is distraction and worry". This is like what *Tejabindu Upanishad* says. According to it that *Āsana* is proper which makes possible continuous *dhyāna* of Brahman.[12] *Āsanas* can be divided into two types: those which are useful in *Prāṇāyāma*, *Dhyāna* and in concentration. The other types are those which are useful in curing bodily ailments and are good for health, such as *Śīrshāsana, Sarvāṅgāsana*.[13] We find that *Śiva-Saṃhitā* recommends four of the more important of the eighty-four *āsanas* viz. *Siddhāsana, Padmāsana, Ugrāsana* and *Swāstika āsana* and describes each of them (III.85-97). Each of these four *āsanas* has its own merit. According to it through the first a *yogī*, at the time of his death attains the *parama gati*, the second helps in making the vital airs equable so that "they flow harmoniously through the body", the third is the bestower of *siddhis* including *vāyu-siddhi*, and the fourth is the giver of good health.[14] *Gheranḍa Saṃhitā*, a well known work on *Haṭha-yoga*, devotes the second *upadeśa* to *āsanas* and describes 32 *āsanas* which are regarded as more useful for mankind.[15]

Prāṇāyāma, says Goraksha, is controlling the flow of *Prāṇa* in the *nāḍis* of the body, and making it steady. The four forms of *Prāṇāyāma*, he says, are *Rechaka* (throwing out the

---

11 *Goraksha Śataka*, vs.11; *Haṭha-Yoga-Pradīpikā* (*HYP*), I, 29, 37.

12 *Tejabindu Upanishad*, p.80 in *Thirty Minor Upanishads*, tr. K.N. Aiyar.

13 *HDS*, V, p.277.

14 *Śiva-Saṃhitā*, III.85-97.

15 *Gheranḍa Saṃhitā*, II.1-43.

air or wind), *Pūraka* (drawing in the air), *Kumbhaka* (retention of breath in the lungs) and the union of *Prāṇa* and *Apāna*.[16] There are three views about the time taken in *Rechaka, Pūraka* and *Kumbhaka*: in proportion 1:4:2 or 1:2:2 or all the three to be of equal duration. The *Purāṇas* have recommended different duration of *mātrās* (time taken in pronouncing a *svara* which is equal to the time taken in touching the little finger by thumb) for *Prāṇāyāma*.[17] It may be pointed out that Patañjali and *Vyāsa Bhāshya* do not use the terms *Rechaka, Pūraka* and *Kumbhaka* but *śvāsa* and *praśvāsa* and *gativichcheda*. Nor *Yoga-Sūtra* says anything about *japa* of Gāyatrī or 'Oṁ' while performing *Prāṇāyāma* unlike the *Smṛitis* and later works. Patañjali has devoted only five *sūtras* to *Prāṇāyāma*. Almost like him, Goraksha in *SSP* has devoted only one verse to this important *aṅga* of *yoga*.[18] In both the instances the object seems to be to indicate the importance of *Prāṇāyāma* leaving the disciple or aspirant to learn it and its various details from a competent Guru, control of *Prāṇa* or vital force of the body being too important a matter.

About *Prāṇāyāma*, Patañjali says that it is "controlling the motion of exhalation and when broken (i.e. held in the lungs)."[19] It may be mentioned that in *Ṛig-Veda*, the word *prāṇa* is used in the sense of breathing when it says that *vāyu* emerged from the *prāṇa* of the Ādi Purusha. In *Taittirīya Saṃhitā*, there is mention of *Prāṇa, Apāna,* and *Vyāna*. *Atharva-veda* mentions *Prāṇas* and *Apānas* (in plural). Also these terms have come in the sense of life. However, there is no mention of *Prāṇayāma* in the earlier *Upanishads* (*Īśa, Kane, Kaṭha, Praśna, Muṇḍa, Māṇḍūkya, Taittirīya,*

---

[16] *SSP*, II.35.

[17] *HDS*, V, p.283.

[18] *Yoga-Sūtra*, II.49-53; *SSP*, II.35; *HDS*, V, pp.385-86.

[19] *Yoga-Sūtra*, II.49.

Chāndogya and *Bṛihadāraṇyaka).* In the *Sūtras*, such as *Āpastamba Dharmasūtra, Gautama Dharmasūtra* and in the same way in *Baudhāyana Dharmasūtra* it is mentioned as a sort of penance. It shows that the concept of *Prāṇāyāma* had so much developed as to be accepted as a religious act, a sort of penance for some acts disapproved by the society but as yet it was not regarded as one of the eight *aṅga* of *yoga.*[20] As Vivekanand observes, *Prāṇa* is not breath, though it is commonly so translated. It is the sum total of cosmic energy "which is in each body and its outward manifestation is the motion of the lungs, which is caused by *Prāṇa* drawing in the breath. We seek to control the breath in *Prāṇāyāma* as the easiest way of getting control of *Prāṇa*, he says,[21] Regarding the types or forms of *Prāṇāyāma, Yoga-sūtra* says (II.50) "Its modifications are either external or internal or motionless, regulated by place, time and number, either long or short".[22] Thus the three kinds of *Prāṇāyāma,* according to it are one by which we draw the breath in, two by which we expel it or throw out and the third is when the breath is held in lungs or stopped from entering the lungs. These are again varied by place (i.e. *prāṇa* is held in some particular part of the body), and time (i.e. how long the *prāṇa* is held or confined).

Chāndogya Upanishad (4/3/3) gives 5 names of *Prāṇa* which on account of their location are termed *Prāṇa, Apāna, Vyāna, Samāna*, and *Udāna*. This shows as Dr. Kane says, that much before the Christian era there was knowledge of the difference in the functions of the five *Prāṇas.*[23]

The result of *Prāṇāyāma* is said to be awakening of the *Kuṇḍalinī*. Also *Prāṇāyāma* removes the covering of *rajas*

---

[20] For a very exhaustive discussion on the use of the words *Prāṇa* and *Prāṇāyāma*, in the *Vedas, Upanishads, Smṛitis, Sūtras*, etc., see Kane, *HDS*, V.pp.278ff.

[21] Vivekanand, *Rāja-Yoga*, 214-15.

[22] *Yoga-Sūtra*, II.50.

[23] *Chāndogya Upanishad*, 4/3/31; Kane, *HDS*, V, p.279.

and *tamas* which cover the *chitta* which otherwise by nature is *sattva* and mind thus becomes fit for *Dhāraṇā* which is the next *aṅga*. Thus in two or three *sūtras*, Patañjali has indicated the main objectives of *Prāṇāyāma*.[24]

Goraksha-Śataka says that by the *Āsanas*, the afflictions of the body are removed while *Prāṇāyāma* destroys the sins and *Pratyāhāra* removes mental *vikāras*. The idea that *Prāṇāyāma* is helpful in destroying the sins has been emphasised in the *Smṛitis* also, such as in Manu (11/248). *Yājñavalkya Smṛiti* (3/305) says that hundred *Prāṇāyāma* wash off even those sins for which there is no provision for *prāyaśchitta*. The importance of *Prāṇāyāma* has been emphasised in many works also. Thus Manu (2/83), Vasishṭha (10/5) and *Vishṇudharma Sūtra* (55/82) say that '*Oṁ*' is *Para-Brahma* and *Prāṇāyāma* is *Parama tapa*.[25]

It may be noted that *Prāṇāyāma* is recognised as one of the limbs in all the forms of *yoga* — *Mantra*, *Haṭha*, *Laya* and *Rāja-Yoga*, though in *Haṭha-yoga* it is regarded as the chief means of attaining *moksha*. It is believed that *vṛittis* or modifications of mind can be brought under control by controlling the *Prāṇa*. A distinction is also made between *sthūla vāyu* (air which is breathed through nose and mouth) and *Prāṇa-vāyu* (*sūkshma-vāyu* or subtle air), the 'vitalising force', and that by controlling the *sthūla-vāyu*, the *Prāṇa-vāyu* can be controlled, and in fact *Prāṇāyāma* really means control of *Prāṇa-vāyu* and not exactly 'breath control', and still more appropriately "the process by which the ordinary and comparatively slight manifestation of *Prāṇa* is lengthened and strengthened and developed",[26] a meaning

---

[24] *Rāja-Yoga*, pp.215-216.

[25] *Goraksha Śataka*, 54; *Manu Smṛiti*, 11/248, 2/83; *Yajñavalkya Smṛiti*, 7/305; *Vishṇu-dharma Sūtra*, 55/82 in *HDS*, V, p.285.

[26] J. Woodroffe, *The Six Centres and the Serpent Power* (*SCSP*), pp.199, 212, 213.

derived from *Prāṇa* and *āyāma*, the latter meaning length, rising. The *Prāṇāyāma* is practiced "to control and develop *Prāṇa*. The latter is then moved into the *Sushumnā* by the stirring of *Kuṇḍalinī* who blocks the entry (*Brahmadvāra*) thereto".[27]

The main object of different forms of *Prāṇāyāma* is to make the *Prāṇa* enter the *Sushumnā* "and then become *Laya* in the *Sahasrāra* after the *Prāṇa-Devatā Kuṇḍalinī* has pierced the intervening *chakras*".[28]

In *Yogamārtanḍa*, while discussing *Prāṇāyāma,* Gorakshanātha says that the period (time taken) of *Uttama Prāṇāyāma* is 36 *mātrās*, of *Madhyama* 24 *mātrās* and of *Adhama* 12 *mātrās*. As a result of the first i.e. *Uttama Prāṇāyāma*, he says, the *mana, buddhi* and *śarīra* (body) become motionless and the *sādhaka* can then control the *Prāṇa*. When performing *Prāṇāyāma*, the work says, the *sādhaka* should meditate on *Praṇava* (*Oṁ*) and that the practice of *Prāṇāyāma* destroys all the sins of a person. The duration of the three types of *Prāṇāyāma* has been put in a different way also. According to it, in *Adhama* it is 4, 16 and 8 (= 28), *Madhyama* is double of that i.e. 8, 32, 16 (= 56) and in *Uttama* it is double of the last viz. 16, 64, 32 (112), the value being measured by the length of *Pūraka, Kumbhaka* and *Rechaka*.[29]

We now come to *Pratyāhāra*, the fifth *aṅga* of *Yoga*. In *SSP, Pratyāhāra*, is explained in this manner. It is, says *SSP,* turning the sense organs away from their respective attractions or weaknesses (*śabda, rūpa, rasa, sparśa, gandha*, etc.) and rid them (sense organs) of the *vikāras* arising from them (II.36).[30] This is very much the same, what Patañjali says, "The drawing in of the organs is (possible) by

---

[27] *Ibid.*, p.213.
[28] *Ibid.*
[29] *Yoga-Mārtanḍa*, VI.92-95; J. Woodroffe, *SCSP*, p. 216.
[30] *SSP*, II.36.

their giving up their own objects of attraction (*sva-vishaya*); when the *chitta* is restrained the sense organs dissociate from their respective *vishaya* and they too are brought under control.[31] *Pratyāhāra* is restraining of the external activity of the sense organs — smell, taste, seeing, feeling and hearing. As a result of *Pratyāhāra*, mind becomes free from the control of the sense organs and mind can be concentrated on any object.

"*Pratyāhāra* is *prati* + *āhāra. Prati* means *pratīpa* i.e. in a reverse direction, *āhāra* means taking away. So *pratyāhāra* is taking away the senses or the mind (*chitta*) in the reverse direction". Khsemarāja describes it as "turning back the individual mind to the universal consciousness from which it has wandered away".[32] *Gheranḍa Saṃhitā* says that by *Pratyāhāra*, all the passions like lust etc., are destroyed by bringing the *chanchala* (wild) *chitta* under control by withdrawing it, whenever it wanders away drawn by various objects of sight etc. It further says that one should withdraw his mind from praise or censure, good or bad speech, pleasant or unpleasant smell, sweet or bitter taste etc.[33] *Kūrma Purāṇa* (2/11/38) briefly puts the same idea and describes *Pratyāhāra* as controlling the sense organs which are naturally attracted towards their respective *vishaya*.

As a result of *Pratyāhāra*, "arises supreme control of the organs", as Patañjali says.[34] Commenting on this observation Vivekānand says, "When the *yogī* has succeeded in preventing the organs from taking the form of external objects (form is not in the object, it is in the *chitta*) and in making them remain one with the mind-stuff, then comes perfect control of the organs".[35] The idea or implied meaning is that

---

[31] *Yoga-Sūtra*, II.54-55; *Rāja-Yoga*, pp.216-17.

[32] *Śiva Sūtras*, p.145, n.4.

[33] *Gheranḍa Saṃhitā (GhS)*, IV.1, 3-5.

[34] *Yoga-Sūtra*, II.55.

[35] *Ibid.*, II.55; *Rāja-Yoga*, 217.

when *chitta* is withdrawn from their respective *vishayas* or objects of the sense-organs, then the sense organs too are dissociated from them. And when the *chitta* is under control then the sense-organs along with *chitta* do not take any cognizance of those objects.

These five external *aṅga* of *yoga* are indirectly helpful in attaining *Saṃprajñāta Samādhi*. We now come to the remaining three *aṅgas* viz., *Dhāraṇā, Dhyāna* and *Samādhi*, which are called *antaraṅga*, but in *Asaṃprajñata Samādhi*, even these three are *bahiraṅga* or external.

How does Gorakshanātha take up these three *aṅga* or stages of *yoga* which are taken as a whole, and in all the three mind is focused on a single or same object. These three *antaraṅga aṅgas* which act internally are taken up by the *sādhaka* one after the other. As usual Gorakshanātha comes to the main point. He says that to establish in one's heart that the same *nija-tattva-svarūpa* (*ātmā* or soul) pervades inside and outside the body and to meditate upon I-consciousness which is like unwavering light of a lamp undisturbed by *vāyu*, is the *lakshaṇa* of *Dhāraṇā*.[36] In *Yogamārtanḍa*, Goraksha says that one should practice *Dhāraṇā* sitting in the appropriate *āsana* after performing *Prāṇāyāma* and equipping oneself with *Pratyāhāra*, closing all the ten outlets of the sense organs, and with ambrosia secreted from the *Sahasrāra* in one's throat, all the five kinds of *Dhāraṇās* are accomplished.[37] In *Gorakshapaddhati* are described these five kinds of *Dhāraṇās* namely *Pṛithvī Dhāraṇā*, *Vāruṇī* (water) *Dhāraṇā*, *Agneyī* (fire) *Dhāraṇā*, *Vāyavī* (*vāyu tattva*) *Dhāraṇā* and *Nabho* (*ākāśa*) *Dhāraṇā*.[38] *Dhāraṇā*, according to Patañjali's *Yoga-Sūtra*, is holding the mind on to a particular place, object or point either in the body or outside the body (such

---

[36] *SSP*, II.37.

[37] *Yoga-Mārtanḍa*, vss.136-55.

[38] *Goraksha Paddhati*, II.52-59.

as symbols, images of Gods and Goddesses), for a predetermined period so that mind starts receiving "the sensations only through that part of the body and through no other part". By fixing the mind on some point or object, the *vikalpas* of the mind begin to dissolve. A *Rāja-Yogī* "gradually effectively practices two kinds of *Dhāraṇā* viz., *Prakṛityāśraya* and *Brahmāśrya*, dependent on the nature or Brahman respectively".[39] It is in a way a prelude to the absorption in the essential Self.

Dhyāna is the seventh *aṅga* and follows *Dhāraṇā*. Gorakshnātha says that one should meditate upon *advaita svarūpa* of Paramātman, the Supreme Soul which is beyond name and form. *Ātmā* is non-different from Him, he says, and one should feel the presence of *Ātma-svarūpa* in all things one beholds, in all living things, and keep *samadrishṭi* or undifferentiated attitude towards all.[40] In *Yogamārtanḍa*, Gorakha dwells at length on the various objects on which *dhyāna* should be concentrated.[41] In *Śvetāśvatara Upanishad* and *Bhagavad-gītā*, there is mention of *Dhyāna-yoga*.

As noted, *Dhyāna* is the second stage after *Dhāraṇā* for attaining *samādhi*. The *Upanishads* have also laid great emphasis on *Dhyāna*. Thus *Māṇḍūkya Upanishad* says that one should meditate upon *Ātmā* in the form of 'Oṁ', and *Viśṇudharma Sūtra* says that one should meditate on the all knowing, omnipotent God who is above the three *guṇas sattva, rajas, tamas*, the 24 *tattvas*, and beyond the knowledge of the sense organs (*indriyātīta*). Gorakha, as noted, also says that one should meditate upon the *advaita svarūpa* of Paramātman. He does not mention *saguṇa dhyāna* which is approved by *Visūṇudharma Sūtra* in case of those who may find it difficult to meditate on *nirguṇa* or *nirākāra*

39 *Yoga-Sūtra*, III.1; *Rāja-Yoga*, 218.
40 *SSP*, II.38.
41 *Yoga-Mārtanḍa*, vss.156-75.

Brahman.[42] According to the *Gheranḍa-Saṃhitā*, *dhyāna* or meditation is of three kinds: (1) *Sthūla* or gross, (2) *Jyotir*; (3) *Sūkshma*. In the first "the Devatā is brought before the mind. In *Jyotir dhyāna*, the *sādhaka* meditates upon *Tejomaya* Brahman, or between the eye-brows on the *Prāṇavātmaka* flame. In *Sūkshma dhyāna*, the *sādhaka* in *Śāṁbhavī-mudrā* meditates on *Kuṇḍalinī*. By this *yoga*, the *ātmā* is revealed, it says.[43]

In the state of *Dhyāna*, there is no consciousness of any effort to concentrate mind on a particular symbol or object while in the *Dhārṇā* such consciousness is present. But in *Dhyāna*, duality (*dvaidha*) exists between the *yogī* or *kartā* and the object or *vishaya* of *Dhyāna*. The two have not merged as yet.

In *Samādhi*, "*dhyāna* reaches that level or stage when there is consciousness of only the object or *dhyeya* and there is consciousness of none other, even of the act of meditating on an object, as the *kartā* is completely absorbed within the *dhyeya* (object of meditation) and there is no longer any *dvaidha* (duality or separation) between the *kartā* and the *dhyeya*.[44] Patañjali in his cryptic *sūtra* style says, "What that, giving up all forms, reflects only on the meaning, it is *samādhi*". Thus, in the state of *Samādhi*, there is no consciousness of any form (and only meaning remains in the mind) and there is total absorption of the self-consciousness in the Supreme Consciousness or Supreme Spirit and there is no consciousness of separateness between the *dhyānakartā* and the object of meditation or *dhyeya*.[45] As *Vishṇu Purāṇa* says, in *Samādhi*, as a result of *dhyāna* or meditation, one is established in the true *svarūpa* of Paramātman and there is no

---

[42] *Māṇḍūkya Upanishad*, 2/2/6; *Vishṇudharmasūtra*, Adh.97 in *HDS*, V, p.289.

[43] *GhS*, VI.1-22; J. Woodroffe, *SCSP*, p.218.

[44] *HDS*, V, p.290.

[45] *Yoga-Sūtra*, III.3; *Rāja-Yoga*, pp.218-19.

consciousness of any separateness between the object of meditation (*dhyeya*), *dhyāna karma* (act of meditation) and the *dhyāna kartā* i.e. the person who is meditating.[46]

Gorakshanātha says that the *lakshaṇa* of *samādhi* is when all *tattvas* are naturally in a fixed or firm condition. In the state of *samādhi*, he says in *Yogamātaṅḍa*, all organs of the body are totally concentrated on the *parama jyoti*. Hence, when the movement of *Prāṇa-vāyu* is no longer felt, the *sādhaka* should try to behold that *parama jyoti*. By practicing *Samādhi*, he says, one attains *moksha*.[47] *Goraksha Paddhati* says that in the state of *samādhi*, the *yogī* realises the *Parama-tattva*, which is eternal, *nirālamba*, *nīrākara*, *nirāshraya* and free from all dualities.[48]

Haṭha Yoga Pradīpikā describes *Samādhi* as the state of non-difference between *Jīvātmā* and *Paramātmā* and in which *chitta* is free from all *saṃkalpas*.[49] Patañjali says: "Among the various *chittas* (minds), that which is attained by *samādhi* is desireless". This is further explained in the next *sūtra* which says that the actions, and the *karmas* produced by those actions, do not bind a *yogī* who has attained perfection, because he did not desire any thing in return.[50] Gorakshanātha does not dwell on the details concerning *Samādhi*, its different types, leaving to a *sadguru* to enlighten his disciple on these points, which are discussed in some other *yoga* works. However, to put briefly *Samādhi* is of two types — *Saṃprajñāta* and *Asaṃprajñāta*. The former can be classified into different categories — *Savitarka, Nirvitark, Suvichāra, Nirvichāra.*

Asamprajñāta Samādhi is attained "by the constant practice of cessation of all mental activity, in which the *chitta*

---

[46] *Vishṇu Purāṇa*, 6/7/92; *HDS*, V, p.290.
[47] *SSP*, II.39; *Yoga-Mārtanḍa*, vss.102-105.
[48] *Goraksha Paddhati*, II.92.
[49] *HYP*, IV, 7.
[50] *Yoga-Sūtra*, IV.6; *Rāja-Yoga*, pp.253-54.

retains only the unmanifested impressions" (*Yoga-Sūtra*, I.18). Commenting in this *Sūtra*, Viekānand says that this *Samādhi* gives us freedom as the mind succeeds in quelling the waves in the *chtita* destroying the 'seeds' which give rise to different tendencies, good or bad, and the '*ātmā*' is left alone in its own splendour and all delusions come to an end. This is seedless *samādhi*.[51]

Gorakshaśataka, describing the final stage of *Samādhi*, says that a *Yogī* fully established in this *Samādhi* has no consciousness of *gandha, rasa, rūpa, sparsha* (touch) or *svara* nor he feels any difference between him and others.[52]

These are the eight limbs or *aṅga* of *yoga* described by Gorakshanātha in his works. It is very clear from the above account that the *Ashṭāṅga yoga* of Goraksha is deeply steeped in the ancient *yoga* traditions of India traceable, to varying extent no doubt, to the *Vedas, Upanishads, Smṛitis, Purāṇas, Yoga-Sūtra*, and other works which have been appropriately though briefly cited in the above pages. Gorakshanātha never even alluded anywhere that he was deviating from the main spiritual and philosophical traditions of the land or that his thought and philosophy were a kind of protest, not to say of revolt, against the ancient Hindu philosophy and *sādhanā*. As described in a subsequent chapter, he believed in "synthesis of all schools of thought and principles in the same Para-Brahma Sachchidānanda". He says that by synthesising the views of all the different schools of philosophy, the state of *viśrānti* (cessation of *chitta – vrittis*) is achieved and the *yogī* is absorbed in Para-Brahma Parameśvara. He in fact becomes *Brahma svarūpa*.[53]

---

51 *Yoga-Sūtra*, I.18; *Rāja-Yoga*, pp.130-137.

52 *GhS*, vss, 97, 99-100 in *HDS*, V, p.291.

53 *SSP*, VI.69-71; *Bhāratī* (Dec.2004), II, p.13.

Chapter VI

Śiva and Śakti

According to the *Siddha-Siddhānta-Paddhati* (*SSP*), *Nijā Śakti*, which is realisable through one's own experience, is non-different from Parama Śiva, and is wholly independent, unchangeable, eternal, awakened and of the form of Supreme Consciousness. She is self-luminous, beyond destruction, and is the sustainer of the entire universe. She is the proximate cause of all phenomenal things, and can be realised by one's own experience. In her *śuddha rūpa* (pure form), She is indistinguishable from Śiva and is identical with Him. In that state there is perfect identity between Śiva and Śakti, says Gorakshanātha.[1]

The *Nijā Sakti* manifests Herself as *Parā Śakti* at the time of creation. This *Parā Śakti* is of the nature of both *kula* and *akula* (i.e. Śiva and Śakti) and an adept should try to realise Her for attaining the state of *sāmarasya*, says Goraksha.[2]

The *Kula Śakti* manifests Herself in five forms: *Parā, Sattā, Ahaṃtā, Sphuratā* and *Kalā* and pervades the entire universe and is the sustainer and maintainer of the *sṛishṭi*. As *Parā-Śakti* She is present in all phenomenal things, and is self-luminous consciousness and all things are manifested by Her.[3] In her *Sattā* form, She is existing since eternity, totally undifferentiated from Parama Advaita Śiva.[4] In Her *Ahaṃtā* form, *Kula Śakti* is eternal, *aprameya* or unfathomable by the

---

1 *Siddha-Siddhānta-Paddhati* (*SSP*), IV.1-2.

2 '*Ibid.*, IV.2.

3 *Ibid.*, IV.3-4.

4 *Ibid.*, IV.5.

sense-organs, self-luminous and is of the form of Sachchidānanda. In Her *Ahaṃtā* form also, She manifests Her non-difference from Śiva. *Kula Śakti* in this *Ahaṃtā* form is also called *Parāhantā*, says *SSP*. In Her *Sphuratā* form, *Kula Śakti* manifests the delightful self-expression of the transcendental spirit in non-dual state. In the form of *Kalā*, She illuminates the true nature of Self, the *ātmā*, which is eternal, self-luminous, imperishable, *nirañjana* and realisable by self-experience.[5]

We have noted that according to Gorakshanātha, *Parā Śakti* is of the nature of both *kula* and *akula*. In the *akula* state, he says, *Parā Śakti* is non-different from Akula Śiva, the eternal Para Brahma Supreme Being (Parameśvara) Ādinātha who is without form (*nirākāra*) and realisable only through self-experience. She constantly remains immanent in Him.[6] *Kula* is the state in which Śiva and Śakti remain in "indistinguishable unity. *Akula* is a state of Śiva different from it. Secondly, *Kula* means body. *Akula* means that of which the body is the letter 'a' (which is the expression of *Chit-Śakti*)". As Jaideva Singh writes "there is double entendre in the word *akula*. It is impossible to bring this out in the translation".[7]

In the *akula* state, says Gorakshanātha, *Parā Śakti* is free from all ties and beyond all phenomenal differences and divisions and is immanent in *Akula* Śiva. In this state, She is *akhaṇḍa* (undivided), incomparable, has no other object, free from cause-effect aspect, and beyond name or form.[8]

According to *SSP*, this *Parā Śakti* which is of the form of *Kulā Śakti* is always ready, ever since having acquired the state of *akula* to reveal Her absolute non-difference and complete identity with Śiva, being in the state of *sāmarasya*.[9]

---

[5] *Ibid.*, IV.6-8.

[6] *Ibid.*, IV.9.

[7] *Śiva-Śūtras*, p.110.

[8] *SSP*, IV.9.

[9] *Ibid.*, IV.10.

This very Śakti is also known as *Aparamparā*, *Nijā* etc., and is the maintainer of the entire universe, of all the diversities of the visible world which are but Her self-manifestation. She is also known as *Ajñāvatī-Śakti* (of Ādinātha).[10] This is what Zimmer says "the cosmic vision of the Tantras which perceives the world as the multitudinous unfolding of the divine energy (Śakti) into a world rich in manifestation".[11]

In the whole of universe, says Gorakshanātha, only Śiva manifests as *kula* and *akula*. At the time of the dissolution of the Cosmic order, Śakti, which is non-different from Śiva, is said to be in the *akula* state. In this state, She is completely non-different from the Highest Reality, the Parama-Tattva, Śiva. In *Kaula-jñāna-nirṇaya*, Gorakshanātha's Guru, Matsyendra, says the same thing in this manner: "At the time of dissolution, Śakti merges in Śiva who Himself then merges in *Kriyā Śakti*. *Kriyā* and *Ichchā Śakti* (the two aspects of Śakti) merge into *Jñāna Śakti*. In this state Śiva (Parama Śiva) alone remains and the world comes to an end".[12]

At the time of the creation (of *sṛishṭi*) *Nijā Śakti* as *Kula Śakti* appears in different forms such as *Parā, Aparā, Sūkshmā* and in Her other forms, as mentioned earlier, for the creation of the universe, and thus She is the source of the entire universe. Even in this state She is neither *dvaita* (*kula*) nor *advaita* (*akula*). Just as the bubbles of water are non-different from water, says *SSP*, by the same logic *Kula-Akula Śakti* is non-different from Śiva. This non-difference, which is beyond duality and non-duality is *sāmarasya*, says Goraksha.[13]

Hence, though non-dual, indivisible Para Brahma with infinite power manifests Himself in diverse forms, and this is the popular perception of the common folk of the world, says

---

[10] *Ibid.*

[11] Zimmer, p.24.

[12] *Kaula-Jñāna-Nirṇaya* (*KJN*), *Paṭala* II.6-7.

[13] *SSP*, IV.11.

Goraksha, but in reality He alone is the sustainer of all phenomenal things. The identity of Śiva and Śakti is eternal, he says, His manifestation in infinite diversity is like the foam and the waves of the sea which are really non-different from the sea water. In the end we find that there is nothing but the Supreme Reality, eternal, omnipresent, Divine, undivided, manifesting in the form of *Kula Śakti*.[14]

Thus, says Gorakshanātha, on account of His being endowed with all the *Śaktis*, Ādinātha Śiva is the source of all phenomenal things. As Absolute Consciousness (*Chit-svarūpa*), He is present in all things. With Śakti immanent in Him, He is capable of doing anything and everything. He is *sarva samartha*. But bereft of Śakti, He can do nothing. Only when He has His *Nijā Śakti* with Him, He is Universal Consciousness and the chief cause (*parama kāraṇa*) of the manifestation of this *Pañchabhautika Jagat,* says Goraksha, emphasising the essential unity of God and the universe.[15]

The same idea is propounded in many other works. In *Kaula-jñāna-nirṇaya* Matsyendranātha (Gorakshanāth's *guru*), says "There is no Śiva without Śakti, nor any Śakti separate from Śiva just as fire and smoke or tree and its shadow cannot exist separately".[16] And it has been said in the *Śiva-Sūtras*, "The *Parā Śakti* (Highest *Śakti*) is only my *ichchā* (will) inseparable from me. She should be considered as natural to me. She is to be known in the same relation to me as heat to the fire, rays to the sun. That Śakti is the cause of the entire world".[17]

Here it may be pointed out that "Śiva and Śakti should not be taken in reality as representing the male and female, as is

---

[14] *Ibid.*, IV.12.

[15] *Ibid.*, IV.13. The above account in *SSP* is a bit complex and may appear repetitive but it is being given as such, as it forms a very important part of their *Śiva-Śakti* doctrine. Later, we have made an attempt to understand it, or at least a part of it, in the light of comparatively modern scientific knowledge.

[16] *KJN*, XVII, 8-9.

[17] Kshemarāja, quoting *Mṛityunjaya*, *Śiva-Śūtras*, p.55.

generally supposed", writes S.N. Dasgupta, "for they are styled as male and female only to please the popular imagination as a mere linguistic expression". In support of the above he cites *Gandharva Tantra* which says, "Śakti, Maheśvara and Brahman, all three signify the same meaning. Their distinction as male, female or neutor is merely due to linguistic usages".[18]

Parameśvara, the Supreme Being, with *Parāpara Śakti* immanent in Him, says Goraksha, is omnipotent, sustainer of the entire universe and is *Viśvarūpa* and *Viśvamaya.*[19]

Here we may consider in brief three different concepts of Primal Energy, as *Prakṛiti, Māyā* and *Śakti* of Sāṃkhya, Vedānta and the Āgama respectively. All agree that the universe is created by the association of a Spirit (called *Purusha, Brahman* and *Śiva* in Sāṃkhya Vedānta and Āgama respectively) and Mind, Matter, Consciousness (termed *Prakṛiti, Māyā* and *Śakti* respectively in the aforesaid systems of thought. They all agree that the first principle is "infinite formless consciousness" and the second is "a *finitising* principle which makes forms ... However, the classical Sāṃkhya posits a plurality of *Ātmans* representing the formless consciousness, with one unconscious *Prakṛiti* which is formative activity. *Prakṛiti* is thus a real independent principle". But Vedāntic monism says that they cannot exist as two independent Realities and that there is only one Brahman. Vedantic monism and the Śaiva-Śakta Āgamas agree that there is one Brahman which has two aspects — transcendent and creative. But whereas according to Śaṃkara, in one aspect (as Para-Brahman) Brahman is dissociated with Māyā and in another (Īśvara aspect) associated with *Māyā* (which is *mithyā* i.e. not real). But how can it be called unreal "when it is the cause of and is empirical experience". Also

[18] *Philosophical Essays*, p.166.

[19] *SSP*, IV.14.

Māyā, though not forming part of Brahman is yet "inseparably associated and sheltered with Brahman in its Īśvara aspect". *Māyā*, like the Sāṃkhya *Prakṛiti*, is not an independent principle. The universe emerged by the reflection of consciousness (Brahman) in unconscious (*Māyā, Prakṛiti*) making unconscious to appear as conscious (*chidā bhāsa*). As Woodroffe says "the positing of *Māyā* at all in this form gives to Saṃkara's doctrine a tinge of dualism from which the Śākta doctrine is free". According to Śaiva-Śāktra doctrine, Śiva and Śakti are one, indistinguishable from each other. So when Śākta Tantra says that all is Brahman, it means it literally. In Para Brahman state, Śakti is not operating but is pure consciousness (*chidrūpiṇī*). In Īśvara aspect of Śiva, "Śiva associated with *Māyā-Śakti*, is the source of movement and change". In different forms, the same *chid-rūpa Śakti* operates and, whether in latent state or in its dynamic aspect, it is always Consciousness. "There is no unconscious *Māyā* which is not Brahman and yet not separate from Brahman". Nor there is any need of *chidābhāsa* which assumes the Brahman and unconscious *Māyā* in which the former reflects itself. In *Āgamas*, Śiva and Śakti are one, Śiva representing the static aspect of the Supreme Power and Śakti the dynamic aspect; "The one Śiva is both the changeless Parā Śiva and Parā Śakti".[20]

It is in this manner that the apparent duality of the Nātha philosophy and the Tantras in general is different from that of Sāṃkhya or Nyāya or Vaiśeshika as here the Lord Śiva is non-different from His Śakti. And it is also different from the unity of the Vedāntists according to whom *ahaṃ* (ego) springs out of the unification of the Brahman with *māyā* since there "... *māyā* is conceived as unreal and so the unity is also unreal."[21]

The above brief discussion about the different views

[20] J. Woodroffe, *Śakti and Śākta* (*JWSS*), pp.210-13.

[21] *Philosophical Essays*, p.160.

regarding the nature of the second principle (*Prakṛiti, Māyā, Śakti* of the Sāṃkhya, Vedānta and Āgama respectively) explains to some extent the reason of Gorakshanātha's great emphasis on the need to understand the Śiva-Śakti doctrine. He further says that *Parāpara Śakti*, in the form of *Kuṇḍalinī*, is present in the individual bodies and it is with Her help that the Siddhas acquire *Kāyā-siddhi*.[22]

We first take up *Siddha-Siddhānta-Paddhati*'s account of the *Kuṇḍalinī Śakti*. According to it, *Kuṇḍalinī Śakti* is of two types — *prabuddha* and *aprabuddha* or *supta*. corresponding to the dynamic and static aspect of *Śakti*. Though She is by nature *chetana svarūpa* but till She is awakened, the worldly people remain bound with afflictions, delusions and worry. She lies asleep at the *Mūlādhāra*, but when awakened rises upwards and on reaching the *Sahasrāra*, rids the *yogīs* of their mental *vikāras*.[23]

Different scholars have tried to understand and interpret the concept of *Kuṇḍalinī Śakti* in different ways. Thus, according to Brahma, "The *Kuṇḍalinī Śakti* is the expression used by the Tantras to indicate the Spiritual Power or Energy of individual human being. In the worldly individual, this Spiritual Power sleeps; it is awakened or becomes active through *sādhanā* or regulated effort to arouse and intensify the spiritual energy that is latent in every man. The individual becomes the Absolute, the *Jīva* becomes Śiva (*Kulārṇava*, IX.42), when the lower self of man realises the higher being and becomes identified with the Higher Self. This is the same as the *Upanishad* view that the Brahman or the Highest is one's own Self (*ātman*)."[24]

Another view is that *Śakti* "when manifesting divides itself into two polar aspects — static and dynamic, which implies that we cannot have it in a dynamic form without at the

---

[22] *SSP*, IV.14.

[23] *Ibid.*

[24] N.K. Brahma, *Philosophy of Hindu Sādhanā* (*PHS*), p.277.

same time having it in a static form, much like the poles of a magnet". When we say *Śakti* is asleep or resting, reference is to the static background of the *Śakti*. As we will see later, the static or potential *Śakti*, by *Prāṇāyāma*, and other yogic practices is activated (roused from sleep as the *Tantras* say) and when it becomes dynamic it begins to move up till it reaches *Sahasrāra* when "the polarisation of the body gives way ... the two poles are untied in one and there is the State of consciousness called *samādhi*". The dynamic form of the *Kuṇḍalinī* is described as "the working force of the body as *Prāṇa*."[25]

Reverting back to Gorakshanātha's account of the Kuṇḍalinī, he says, She is the seed of all manifestation. The sky and the entire physical creation, emanate from Her. Being *Parama sattā*, exercising control over every body, She is of the form of *Vimarśa-rūpinṇī-vidyā*. By *sādhanā* of *Kuṇḍalinī*, *yogī* easily realises the true nature of Self (*ātma-svarūpa*), says Goraksha.[26]

Although *Kuṇḍalinī Śakti* is essentially the same, continues Goraksha, She is called *adhaḥ* when She is in the *Mūlādhāra chakra*, *Madhya Śakti* when in the *Maṇīpūra chakra* in the navel region, and *Ūrdhva Śakti* when She is in the *Sahasrāra dala*. By attracting *Ūrdhva Śakti* upwards and by Her *nipāta-saṃyojana*, *Paramapada* is realised. Thus, though *Kuṇḍalinī Śakti* is essentially one, She is given three different names depending on Her position during Her ascent to the transcendental spiritual plane to be untied with the Supreme Spirit.[27]

So long as *Kuṇḍalinī Śakti* lies asleep, continues *SSP*, the *sādhaka* is afflicted by worries and worldly matters. The *Yogī* by expansion and contraction of this *Śakti* in the *Mulādhāra*

---

[25] *JWSS*, p.444.

[26] *SSP*, IV.15.

[27] *Ibid.*, IV.16-17.

where She lies 'asleep', and by *Mūlādhāra bandha, Uḍḍiyāna bandha* and *Jālandhara bandha*, by uniting *Prāṇa* and *Apāna vāyus*, makes *Kuṇḍalinī* to rise upwards and secure to the adept the highest bliss. The *Kuṇḍalinī Śakti*, when in the *Mūlādhāra*, is the *Mūla Śakti*, says *SSP*, and by Her contraction and expansion causes creation and destruction of the universe. *Kuṇḍalinī* as *Madhya Śakti* being *chidrūpa* is the real *svarūpa* of the *Jivātmā*.[28] This *Kuṇḍalinī Śakti* is also described as of two types — *sthūla* and *sūkshma*. When present in the *Mūlādhāra*, She is too subtle and beyond the comprehension of the worldly people. Since She creates the gross visible world, She is known as *Sṛishṭi Kuṇḍalinī*. The same *Śakti* by her power to expand moves up from the navel region and by her *chaitanya svarūpa* reveals to the *yogīs* Her true nature — blissful, omniscient, undivided soul.[29] Explaining vs.3 of *Vijñānabhairva*, Jaideva Singh writes that when *Kuṇḍalinī* rises in *Sushumnā* and piercing the various *chakras* (centres of energy) finally reaches in *Sahasrāra*, "the yogī experiences spiritual light with which he feels identified. This is what is meant by saying that the divine is revealed by the aid of the interior *prāṇic* force residing in *Sushumnā*".[30]

When *Kuṇḍalinī* moves upwards from the *Nābhi chakra* in Her *akhaṇḍa svarūpa*, continues Gorakshanātha, She is omnipotent, subtle and free from *vyāpti-vyāpaka-bhāva* (feeling of inseparableness and pervasiveness). Hence this subtle *chidrūpiṇi* Madhya Kuṇḍalinī should be awakened for *deha-siddhi* and for manifestation of one's real Self. (IV.23). The entering of *Madhya Kuṇḍalinī* in *Sahasrāra* is called *Ūrdhva Śaktipāta*. It is through the *Ūrdhva Śakti*, which is above all physical manifestations, that one can realise the

---

[28] *Ibid.*, IV.18-20.

[29] *Ibid.*, IV.21-23.

[30] *Vijñānabhairava*, p.32.

Parmapada, says *SSP*, which is of the form of Parameśvara, the Supreme Reality, who is without name or form and is infinite, *akhaṇḍa* Universal Soul. Penetrating *Maṇīpūra* and other *chakras*, *Mahākuṇḍalinī* unites with Śiva in the *Sahasrāra* and ends all differences of He, You and I and reveals the *akhaṇḍa, vyāpaka* (all pervasive) nature of *ātmā* and *Paramātmā* and non-difference between Śiva and Śakti just as Moon and Moon-light are inseparable. The Universal Conscience pervades all orders of existences, all *tattvas*, the entire universe, and it is by the self-unfoldment of His *Śakti* that this Cosmic order is manifested which is but manifestation of Śiva-Śakti.[31] It is for this reason that "human body is conceived as having a very important place and function in the cosmic-self-expression of Śiva Śakti."[32]

There are a few points in the above exposition of the nature of *Kuṇḍalinī Śakti* and Her ascent which can be explained further in a somewhat different way and here we will quote extensively from the works of John Woodroffe and Oscar Marcel Hinze who have sought to understand the Tantric version of the phenomenon of *Kuṇḍalinī* in the light of the modern scientific knowledge without challenging the basic premises of the *Tantras*. We have spoken of the polarisation of Energy (*Śakti*) into static or potential (i.e. *Kuṇḍalinī*) and dynamic (the working force of the body as *Prāṇa*). When *Śakti*, after being made dynamic by *Prāṇāyāma* and other yogic practices, reaches *Sahasrārā*, the two poles are untied and the state of consciousness then is called *Samādhi*.[33]

"The *Śākta Tantra* is a rendering of Vedantik Truth from the practical point of view, and represents the world-process as a polarisation in Consciousness itself. This polarity as it exists in, and as, the body is destroyed by *yoga* which disturbs

---

31 *SSP*, IV.23-29.
32 *PGN*, p.138.
33 *JWSS*, p.445.

the equilibrium of bodily consciousness, which is due to the maintenance of these two poles.[34]

Here it may be mentioned that man being in the fullest sense a microcosm, there is nothing in the universe or macrocosm which is not in the human body, as per the cosmology of the *Tantra yoga*. *Śabda Brahman* is the creator of both. Now the creative power of *Śabda Brahman* is *Mahākuṇḍalinī* in the macrocosm and *Kuṇḍalinī* (said to be coiled up) in microcosm or as John Woodroffe says, *Samashṭi Śakti* (collectivity) in relation to which the *kuṇḍalī* in individual bodies is *Vyasīṭi Śukti*. The body is a microcosm or *Kshudra-brahmāṇḍa*. In the living body, therefore, there is same polarisation. "In the human body, the potential pole of Energy which is the Supreme Power is stirred to action on which the moving forces (dynamic *Śakti*) supported by it are drawn thereto, and the whole dynamism thus engendered moves upward to unite with the quiescent Consciousness in the *Sahasrāra*, the Highest Lotus, which is the other static centre.[35]

"Behind all activity there is a static background. This static centre in the human body is the *Kuṇḍalinī* in *Mūlā-dhāra* (root support) of the whole body". Now Śiva is described as "the unchangeable static aspect of the great Consciousness while Śakti represents the dynamic aspect of the same consciousness". As described earlier it is *Śakti* which creates the five *Mahābhūtas*: *Mahā Ākāśa*, *Mahā Vāyū, Mahā Teja* (Agni), *Mahā Salila*, and *Mahā Pṛithvī*, the first being finest i.e. *Ākaśa* and the last (*Pṛithvī*) being the grossest. By the time the earth element is created, the *Śakti* is believed to have exhausted her creative power to the maximum limit and "she lies rolled together and sleeps", as the Tantras describe. "The six centres are to be considered as the main stages of *Śakti* on

---

34 *Ibid.*, pp.442-443.

35 *Ibid.*, pp.442-44; Hinze, pp.35-36.

her way from the heaven (microcosmically the region of the head, i.e. 1000 petalled lotus) which is the region of pure undimmed consciousness, and is thus the realm of Śiva, which is also the proper home of *Śakti.*"[36]

When "roused up" by the yogic practices it ascends from *Mūlādhāra* to the next higher centre i.e. *Svādhishṭhāna* and then to the following *chakras* or centres in the ascending order. *Maṇīpūra*, *Anāhata* (here the *Śakti* is transformed into sound), *Viśuddha* (here "it becomes a pure *sātvic* element") and *Ājñā*. At this stage the *sādhaka* or practitioner is able to see the *Śakti*, though only for a moment, in the form of a sharp flash of lightning. The passage of the *Kuṇḍalinī* from *Mūlādhāra* to the *Ājñā,* the sixth centre of energy, is said to constitute the first part of Her ascent.

"These centres in the body of man have their correspondence in the cosmic planes, and each of them has its own *guṇa* or quality and a Presiding Deity. When the disciple ascends centre by centre, he passes through the corresponding *Lokas* or cosmic planes". This becomes clear from the following table given by John Woodroffe.

Psychic Centre in Man's body	*Loka* (or Cosmic Plane)	*Guṇa* (Quality)	Presiding Deity
Mūlādhāra	*Bhuvarloka*		
		Tamas	*Agni*
Svādhishṭhāna	*Svarloka*		
Maṇipūra	*Maharaloka*		
		Rajas	Sun
Anāhat	*Janaloka*		
Viśuddh	*Tapoloka*		
		Satva	Moon
Ājnñā	*Satyaloka*		

---

[36] *JWSS*, p.442; Hinze, p.36.

The second part of the ascent is when the *Kuṇḍalinī Śakti* moves up from *Ājñā* to *Sahasrāra*, "In this place live in union", it is said "*Sat* (Sadā-Śiva) and the *chit* (The Absolute, the Consciousness that is the unchanging principle of all changes)". ... *Kuṇḍalinī* which has been led all the way to the *Sahasrāra* should be merged into this union; this is the end of the aspirant's journey, he now enjoys beautitude (*Parmānanda*) itself".

Kuṇḍalinī Śakti, we are told, does not stay for long in the *Sahasrāra* and has a tendency to return to Her original position i.e. *Mūlādhāra*. Hence the process is repeated several times till Śakti makes a permanent stay in the *Sahasrāra*. The aspirant then attains *Jīvana-mukta* stage.

"After union with Śiva, *Kuṇḍalinī* makes her return journey. After She has repeatedly gone to Him, she makes a journey from which, at the will of the *yogī*, there is no return".[37]

During her ascent, the *Kuṇḍalinī* reabsorbs everything that has been created during her earlier desent — first the earth element "which is carried back to its seed-sound *laṁ*, out of which it once originated. This seed-sound will then be dissolved into the element "water" which is again changed in its seed-sound *vaṁ*, which now forms the body of the *Kuṇḍalinī*. When the Śakti climbs up further, the seed sound *vaṁ* is dissolved into the "fire-element" and this again is changed into the sound *raṁ* which at this moment forms the body of the *Kuṇḍalinī*-serpent. Thus it goes on further, not only the elements and seed-sounds but everything that is in the respective lotuses is dissolved", including the differentials of the sounds, the ruling gods, the sense-qualities (smelling, tasting etc.). "All this is re-absorbed by the ascending *Kuṇḍalinī Śakti* who releases herself step by step, until finally

[37] J. Woodroffe, *The Six Centres and the serpent Power* (*SCSP*), pp.248-259, 282-283. mostly based on the *Samaya-Āgamas*.

she unites with Śiva in the 1000 petalled lotus — an event which the *yogī* experiences as the highest ecstasy (*samādhi*)". On account of the process of stepwise dissolution of all creation, in the microcosm, this form of *yoga* is called *Laya Yoga*, *Laya* meaning dissolution," says Hinze.[38]

Hinze writes further in his lucid style "In general, the *yogī* cannot remain in *samādhi* for a long time: a natural impulse leads the *Kuṇḍalinī Śakti*, again, step by step below so that little by little the re-absorbed worlds are newly created. .... While the great *Śakti* cramps herself step by step on her way from the heaven to the earth, the macrocosmic and the microcosmic "worlds" arise. When, on the other hand, that Śakti, through the method of *Yoga*, wakes up from her *Kuṇḍalinī*-state and ascends upwards, releasing herself little by little, the worlds are bound to disappear in the same degree ..."[39]

The above account helps to some extent in understanding what Gorakshanātha meant by saying that the entire physical creation emanates from *Kuṇḍalinī Śakti*, the description of Her ascent, and what is meant by stating that the *Kuṇḍalinī* lies at the *Mulādhāra chakra* asleep like a serpent coiled three times and a half till She is awakened.

There is yet another description of the process of the awakening of the *Kuṇḍalinī Śakti* and her ascent upwards in the *Sushumnā*. According to it *Śakti* (Energy) as manifesting itself in the universe divides itself into two polar aspects: static *Kuṇḍalinī Śakti* at rest or "coiled" and dynamic *Prāṇa* diffused all over the body in a condition of equilibrated energy. The rousing of *Kuṇḍalinī* from 'sleep' involves application of the diffused dynamic power i.e. *Prāṇa* by withdrawing it (partially) and converging it along the axis ... so that diffused *Prāṇa* has now both magnitude and direction.

---

[38] Hinze, p37 and n.39.

[39] *Ibid.*, p.39.

It is suggested that it could also be "a partial conversion of the infinite coiled power into a sort of influence that can thus gather the diffused *Prāṇa* and converge it on its own resultant line along the axis, or an inductive action, analogous to electro-magnetic action by which the *Prāṇas* are collected and converged". In *Yogic* treatises we are told that by certain *yogic* practices, the *Prāṇa-vāyu* is made to enter *Sushumnā* and *Prāṇa* and *Kuṇḍalinī Śakti* then begin their upward journey to *Sahasrāra*.[40]

Other aspects related to *Kuṇḍalinī* and Her ascent have been discussed at many other places, such as when discussing the evolution of *Para-Piṇḍa*, *Nāḍīs*, *Nāda*, *Samādhi, Mudrās* and *Bandha*, *chakras*, *Praṇāyāma*, etc. That *Kuṇḍalinī* figures so prominently in the *Tantras* is not surprising as the idea of *Kuṇḍalinī* is fundamental to *Haṭha-yoga*. As *Haṭha-Yoga-Pradīpikā* says, all the *Tantras* and *yoga*-practices rest on *Kuṇḍalinī* just as Śeshanāga is the support of the earth with all the mountains etc.

---

[40] *SCSP*, p.313.

Chapter VII

Paramapada, Sāmarasya, Sahaja-Jñāna and the role of Sadguru

Gorakshanātha in *Siddha-Siddhānta-Paddhati* says that after acquiring knowledge of the individual body (*vyashṭi-piṇḍa*) and the cosmic body (*Para-piṇḍa*), one should establish *sāmarasya* (identity) with *Paramapada Paramātmā*, the Supreme Spirit.[1]

Paramapada, says Goraksha, is realisable only by deep meditation and reflection, and by direct transcendental experience.[2] It is important that "the idea of the body being the Self disappears to be steeped in the ..... pure consciousness". *Paramapada* is self-luminous, he says, and does not become manifest by any other light (of knowledge). It is beyond the power of the intellect to know Him, nor the mind can reach Him, nor speech can describe Him, however rich and adoring may be the language used, nor even an eloquent *guru* can describe His *tattvas* (constitutive principles and elements). And that is why Śiva Himself has described Him as *svasaṃvedya* i.e. one who can be perceived or known by oneself. Even scholars, continues Goraksha, who have acquired mastery in the exposition of subtle ideas are

---

[1] *Siddha-Siddhānta-Paddhati (SSP)*, V, vs.1.

[2] *Sadgurus* are of two types. Those to whom *Jñāna* comes by itself, its extent depending upon that of the *śaktipāta*. *Guru* who receives *Jñāna* from another *Guru* is a *Saṃskṛita Guru*. When a disciple is initiated by a *Sadguru*, *Jīva* acquires *tattva-jñāna* or *Brahma-Jñāna* and becomes *jīvana-mukta* (*Tāntrika Sādhanā aur Siddhānta*, p.96). Here *Jñāna* is interpreted as *svarūpa-jñāna* or knowledge of Self.

perplexed when describing *Paramapada*. He has to be sought and searched. He cannot be attained with the help of (objective) proofs. He is realisable by direct transcendental experience, and only by the grace of a *sadguru* (self realised spiritual teacher).[3]

According to Gorakshanātha, intensive awareness and mental observation of one's own true nature (knowledge of Self) leads to the recognition of the non-difference between one's own individual body and the Supreme Cosmic body, inhering the attributes of each of the five Divine *Śaktis*, *Nijā, Parā, Aparā, Sūkshmā* and *Kuṇḍalinī*, and one sees the Supreme Being (Parameśvara) established in his own Self. This experience of complete non-difference between the individual body (*sva-pinḍa*) and Supreme Cosmic body (*Para-pinḍa*) leads to the state of *Nirutthāna* or *Sāmarasya* (absorption in the Universal Consciousness). This experience of the individual soul (*Jivātmā*), which is of the form of Sachchidānanda *Svarūpa* consisting of existence, thought and joy, leads to *ātma-bodha* or knowledge of one's true nature (*ātma-jñāna*) or *svarūpa-jñāna* (knowledge of Self) and non-difference between the *Jivātmā* and the Paramātmā. This ends the feeling of duality between the individual body and the cosmic body, says Gorakshanātha, and *Paramapada*, the undivided, self-luminous Universal Consciousness manifests in all its transcendent glory.[4]

We may note that Gorakshanātha lays great emphasis on the ideal of *Samarasakaraṇa* or absorption in the Supreme

---

[3] *Ibid.*, V. vss.2-6.

[4] *Siddha-Siddhānta-Paddhati*, V. vss.7-8. The *Vajrayāni Siddha* Sarahapāda describes *Paramapada* as beyond *Dvaita, Advaita* or *Vishishṭādvaita*, without beginning or end, beyond the reach of *mana, pavana*, sun or moon. On realising *Paramapada*, *Jīva* perpetually experiences the highest bliss and happiness. Sarah uses *Sahaja, Mahāsūkha* and *Paramapada* as conveying the same meaning. *Dohākośa*, 29-38, *Vajrayānī Siddha Sarahapāda*, pp.173-174.

Consciousness. Is *Samarasakaraṇa* a stage higher than *Samādhi*? In the state of *Samādhi* also, as *Haṭha-Yoga Pradīpikā* says, there is realisation of complete non-difference between *Jivātmā* (individual soul) and Paramātmā (Universal Soul) and complete dissolution of all the *saṃkalpas* and absorption of individual consciousness in the Universal Consciousness just as salt dissolves in water.[5] According to one view, Gorakshanātha seems to assign to *Samrasakaraṇa* a position superior to that of *Samādhi* which is a condition precedent to the realisation of *Samarasa*, "for the latter implies a permanent illumined spiritual state. .... An enlightened *yogī* who attains the state of *Sāmarasya*, sees and enjoys the differences and at the same time sees and enjoys the internal unity of the differences while living and moving amidst diversities and changes, he always inwardly dwells in the realm of blissful changeless spiritual Unity. He sees and enjoys himself in all and all in himself. Gorakshanātha calls it *Sahaja-Samādhi* and also *Jāgrat-Samādhi* i.e. *Samādhi* in the normal waking state".[6]

Coming back to the *Siddha-Siddhānta-Paddhati*, this awareness of the non-difference between the individual body (*vyashṭi-pinḍa*) and Supreme Cosmic body (*Para-pinḍa*), says Goraksha, is attained by the grace of the *Guru* and for this reason, the *Siddha Yogīs* seek refuge at the feet of a *Sadguru*, and under his direction, and by concentrating on the true nature of Self, and by eliminating *chitta-vṛittis*[7] or mental modifications by practicing *dhyāna* and *smādhi* and *yogic sādhanā*, experience the unity and identity of the individual body and the Supreme Cosmic body, and (thus) realise *Paramapada,* and inhere *Paramapada* in their individual bodies (*vyashṭi-pinḍa*) experiencing the bliss of this identity.[8]

---

[5] *HYP*, IV.7.

[6] *PGN*, pp.246-47.

[7] *Siddha-Siddhānta-Paddhati*, V, vs.10.

[8] *Ibid.*, V, vs.11.

According to the *Mahāsiddhas*, says Goraksha, *Paramapada* is Śiva with *chidrūpa Śakti* inhering in Him.[9]

By the examination of the individual body (*piṇḍa-parīkshā*) is meant to feel the bliss of the light of the Supreme Spirit within the body and then, after gathering this light within oneself, to feel being non-different from the Paramātman (Supreme Soul) or the Universal Consciousness. To experience this non-difference is *sāmarasya*, says Gorakshanātha.[10] As a result of this experience, the body of the *yogī* is filled with a mass of the Great Divine Light (*Mahā-Prakāśa-puñja*) as a result of which he achieves *deha-siddhi* In *deha-siddhi*[11] state, one feels the all pervading presence of the Supreme Soul, and all the *siddhis* present themselves before him.[12]

On realising *Paramapada*, the whole universe is perceived as *Paramātma-svarūpa*. In this state, Gorakshanātha says, the *sādhaka* or adept should not get entangled with the *siddhis*; instead he should give full attention (devotion) to experiencing *Paramapada*.[13]

The Yoga Mārga, Sahaja Jñāna, Saṃyama, and Sopāya: The path of *yoga* or *yoga-mārga*, as noted, is considered to be

---

[9] *Ibid.*, V, vs.25. Cf. *Nirālamba Upanishad* which says that *Paramapada* is the supreme abode of Brahman, far superior to *Prāṇas*, the organs of sense and actions, *chitta*, and is of the nature of *Sachchidānanda.*

[10] *Siddha-Siddhānta-Paddhati*, V. vs.11.

[11] *Kāya-sādhana* is one of the ways to achieve *Deha-siddhi* and is regarded as "an indispensable accessory to the realisation of the *Sahajā* nature or Supreme bliss. (*Obscure Religious Cults*, p.197).

[12] *Siddha-Siddhānta-Paddhati*, V. vss.12, 17.

[13] *Siddha-Siddhānta-Paddhati*, V. vss.18-19. About the rejection of the *siddhis*, Patañjali (*Yoga-sūtra*, IV.28-29) says that a *yogī* who gains knowledge of the true nature of soul acquires all the powers or *siddhis* but a true *yogī* rejects them. To him comes "a peculiar knowledge, a particular light called *Dharma-megha* or the cloud of virtue after which there is no fear of any evils dragging the *yogī* down". To him comes peace and calmness and he becomes totally free from the fear of falling, pain or evil. The *siddhis* are an obstacle to the attainment of the highest goal i.e. attainment of the knowledge of the true Self. (Vivekānand, *Rāja Yoga*, 264-65).

superior to all other paths, and to lend authority to this statement, *Siddha-Siddhānta-Paddhati* says that even Śiva has said the same in *Śrutis, Smṛitis, Tantras* and *Āgamas*. It is superior in the sense that it is bestower of *moksha* and leads to *Paramātma-bodha* or realisation of the Supreme Soul. *Siddha-Siddhānta-Paddhati* says that on attaining *moksha* one is established in *akhaṇḍa-ātma-svarūpa*. The same object of *yoga* is implied in Patañjali's *Yoga-Sūtra* (I.2-4). Here *yoga* has been described as restraining the *chitta-vṛittis*, and when these are controlled (by concentration) says *Sūtra* 3, explaining the object of *yoga*, "the seer (*Purusha*) can see his own true nature which at other times, the seer identifies with the *vṛittis* (modifications). *Gheranḍa Saṃhitā* also says that the *Yoga* leads to the knowledge of truth or *tattva-jñāna* (knowledge of the Reality).[14]

In *Gorakshapaddhati*, Gorakshanātha describes *Yoga-śastra* as a fruit of the *Vedas* which, he says, are like *Kalpavṛiksha*.[15] This is a very significant observation. Eminent scholars like Dr. P.V. Kane have shown that the origin of the *yoga* system can be traced to the *Vedas* and much more clearly in the *Upanishads, Smṛitis, Mahābhārata, Bhagvada-Gītā, Purāṇas,* etc.[16] The observation of Gorakshanātha is also important as we find in some works veiled tendency to underrate the value of the study of the *Vedas*. Thus *Dhyānabindu Upanishad* says that "he is the knower of the *Vedas* who knows the three seats, the three *mātrās*, the three *Brahmās*, the three *aksharas* and the *mātrās* associated with the *ardha-mātrā*. He who knows which is above *bindu, nāda* and *kāla* ... is a knower of *Vedas*",

[14] *Siddha-Siddhānta-Paddhati*, V, vss.20-21; *Yoga-Sūtra*, I.2-3; *Gh.S.*, I.2; *Yājñavalkya Śmṛiti* (1/8) gives highest place to *Yoga* and describes it as an inseparable part of *Vedānta*. It also says that self-realisation (*ātma-darśana*) through *yoga* is the *parama dharma*.

[15] *Gorakshapaddhati*, p.8.

[16] See, P.V. Kane, *HDS*, Vol.V, pp.246-261

implying that their knowledge is the real *Vedas*, and one who knows these is as good as having read the *Vedas*. That knowledge or *jñāna* should be called *Veda* by which one realises the *Paramātmā* (Supreme Soul), it says and *Muṇḍaka-Upanishada* classifies knowledge (*vidyā*) as *Aparā* and *Parā*, and puts the four *Vedas*, as well as *Nirukta*, *Chhanda* and *Jyotish*, in the category of *Aparā-vidyā* and describes *Parā-vidyā* as one which leads to the knowledge of *Akshara Brahman*, the imperishable *avināśī Brahman*.[17] Similarly, it is said that some *Śāstras* are *moksha rakshaka* (protector of *moksha*) like *Yoga-Śāstra* while some are *vyavahāra-rakshaka* (protector of *vyavahāra*) like the *Śruti*, *Smṛitis* etc. It is also said that *Vedas* delineate the *karmas* and so are meant for *karmādhikāris*. The *yogīs* on the other hand renounce the *karmas* and all worldly things. Besides, there are so many differing interpretations of the *Vedas*, *Upanishads*, such as those by Śaṃkara and Rāmānuja. Hence the *yogīs* have little to do with the *Sthūla-Veda*. Their concern is only with *Oṁkāra*, from which all the *Vedas* originated and in which they all end. *Oṁkāra* is the essence of the *Vedas*, and meditating on it even for a moment is as beneficial as performing hundred *yajnas*. It is in the light of the above observations that Gorakshanātha's statement that *Yoga-Śāstra* is the fruit of the *Vedas* becomes important. It may be pointed out that this approach was to some extent due to strong opposition to *Varṇāśrama dharma* which had approval of the *Śrutis*. Thus *Sūtasaṃhitā* says that one who has freed himself from *Varṇāśrama*, is *guru* of the *gurus* and no one is greater than him in the world. And one who has pride of his *Varṇa* is a servant of the *Śṛutis* i.e. he is bound by the bondage of the *Vedas* and one who is free from such pride is the master of the *Śṛutis*. Or such statement as the real *Veda* is the *jñāna* through

---

[17] *Dhyānabindu Upanishad*, pp.204-205 (in *Thirty Minor Upanishads*, tr. K.N. Aiyar); *Muṇḍaka-Upanishad*, 4-5.

which one realises Paramātmā and not the books called *Vedas*.[18] Later we will see that one of the essential prerequisites for being an *Avadhūta* is to be *atyāśramī* i.e. above the four *avasthās* of the system viz. *Brahmacharya, Gṛihastha, Vānaprastha* and *Sanyāsa*, also.[19]

Gorakhanātha goes on to explain the true meaning of *Yoga*. Here *Yoga* does not mean the commonly understood meaning i.e. uniting two things, that meaning is not relevant here. The principal meaning of *yoga* in this context is the knowledge which leads to the attainment of *moksha*,[20] he says.

In *Amaraughaprabodha*, Gorakshanātha says that *yoga* is accepted as of four types — *Laya-yoga, Haṭha-yoga, Mantra-yoga* and *Rāja-yoga*. He is critical of *Pañchamakāra* and other controversial practices indulged in by some of *Haṭha-yogīs* and says that without *Rāja-yoga* one can neither achieve *deha-siddhi* nor *Īśvara-siddhi*. He also describes the four stages of *yoga* which are common in all the types of *yoga* viz. *arambhāvasthā, ghaṭāvasthā, parichayāvasthā* and *nishpattivasthā*.[21]

Śiva-Saṃhitā and *Haṭha Yoga Pradīpikā* (*HYP*) dwell at length on the types of *yoga* and the four stages or *avasthās* in *yoga* and also on the relation between *Haṭha-yoga* and *Rāja-yoga*. *Śiva-Saṃhitā* says (V.9) that the four kinds of *yoga* are *Mantra-yoga, Haṭha-yoga, Laya-yoga* and *Rāja-yoga* (which removes all duality). The *Sādhakas* or

---

18 *Goraksha-Siddhānta-Saṃgraha*, pp.4-5, 15-16, 66.

19 *Siddha-Siddhānta-Paddhati*, VI, vs.21.

20 *SSP*, V.22-23; *Bhāratī*, p.57. In *Rāja-Yoga*, the highest aim is *mukti* from *Prakṛiti* (*Māyā* of *Advaitavādis*). For the *Vedāntists*, says Prof. Kane, *mukti* means absorption in Brahman or *Kaivalya*. The concept of *mukti* in *Siddha-Siddhānta-Paddhati* is similar. *Moksha* in Kashmir Śaivism is recognition of one's true nature or pure I-consciousness. In *Yoga*, it means liberation of *Jīvātmā* from the cycle of birth and re-birth.

21 *Amaraughaprabodha*, vss.3-4, 8, 45.

aspirants suitable for each type of *yoga* are also different and they can be put under four categories: mild (*mṛidu*), moderate (*madhya*), ardent (*dhimātra*) and most ardent (*adhimātra*).[22]

Thus those entitled to *Mantra-yoga* are described as having many shortcomings such as being sickly, lacking enthusiasm, timid, etc., while those entitled to *Laya-yoga*, the moderate ones are liberal minded, forgiving, and who avoid extremes. The ardent ones (*dhimātra*) are more suitable for *Haṭha-yoga*. They are steady minded (*sthira-buddhi*), knowing *Laya-yoga*, energetic, magnanimous, truthful, courageous, full of faith, devoted to their *gurus*, and the most ardent ones are those who are extremely energetic, who know the *Śāstras*, who are fearless, religious, worshipper of God and the *guru*. They are entitled to all the four kinds of *yoga*.[23]

Rāja-yoga is regarded as the highest and most difficult form of *yoga*. It is by means of *Mantra-yoga*, *Haṭha-yoga* and *Laya-yoga* that an adept gradually attains a level of purity which makes him fit for *Savikalpa-Samādhi*, but it is through *Rāja-yoga* alone that one can attain to *Nirvikalpa-Samādhi* in which "there is not the slightest seed of attachment to the world and in which therefore there is no return thereto but eternal unity with the Brahman." In the *samādhi* of *Rāja-yoga* "there is complete *chit-svarūpa-bhāva* and final (*Nirvikalpa*) Liberation".[24]

In the introductory lines, the author of *Gheranḍa-Saṃhitā*, describes *Haṭha-yoga* "as the first rung of the ladder that leads to *Rāja-yoga*,[25] and the author of *Haṭha-yoga Pradīpikā* says that he is composing this work to dispel the confusion about *Rāja-yoga* caused by multiplicity of views. Later he says that

---

[22] *Śiva-Saṃhitā*, V. 9-13. For their respective qualities and shortcomings, see the same work, V.11-14. See also *Amaraughaprabodha*, VI, 18-24.

[23] *Śiva-Saṃhitā*, V. 11-14.

[24] A. Avalon (John Woodroffe), *The Six Centres and the Serpent Power* (*SCSP*), p.254.

[25] *Gheranḍa-Saṃhitā* (*Gh.S*), p.1.

"no success is possible in *Rāja-yoga* without *Haṭha-yoga*, and no success (is possible) in *Haṭha-yoga* without *Rāja-yoga* (as the final objective). One should therefore practice both of these well till complete success is gained. In Canto IV.102 of the work he says that "all the methods (*upāya*) of *Haṭha-yoga* are meant for gaining success in *Rāja-yoga*".[26] *Śiva-Saṃhitā* also says that *Haṭha-yoga* cannot be (obtained) without the *Rāja-yoga* nor can the *Rāja-yoga* be obtained without *Haṭha-yoga*. So let the *yogī* first learn *Haṭha-yoga* under the instructions of a wise *guru*.[27]

These observations show that perfection in *Haṭha-yoga* is a necessary step to gain success in *Rāja-yoga*. *Śiva-Saṃhitā* describes how *Rāja-yoga* is performed. "Let him close the ears with his thumbs, the eyes with the index fingers, the nostril with the middle fingers, and with the remaining four fingers he should press the upper and the lower lips. The *yogī* having thus firmly confined the air, sees his *ātmā* (soul) in the shape of light. Practicing this continually, he loses consciousness of his physical, subtle and causal bodies and becomes one with that soul. He is absorbed in Brahman, and practicing it gradually one begins to hear *Nāda*.[28]

The account given in *Haṭha-Yoga-Pradīpikā* (*HYP*), is perhaps more clear. It says "I will now describe the practice of *Anāhata-nāda* as propounded by Gorakshanātha for the benefit of those who are unable to understand the principles of knowledge i.e. *Śāstras* etc., and that it is the chief among the various methods for going into absorption.

"Sitting in *Muktāsana* with the *Śāmbhavī mudrā*, the *yogī* should hear this sound inside his right ear with collected (concentrated) mind. When the ears, the eyes, the nose and the mouth are closed then a more clear sound is heard in the

---

[26] *Haṭha-Yoga-Pradīpikā* (*HYP*), I.3, II.76, IV.102.
[27] *Śiva-Saṃhitā*, V. 181.
[28] *Ibid.*, V. vss.22-26.

passage of the *Sushumnā* which has been cleaned of its impurities".[29]

Haṭha-Yoga-Pradīpikā then describes the four stages of *yoga* mentioned by Gorakshanātha, as mentioned. But before we proceed further let us know more about the *Śāmbhavī-mudrā* as described by *HYP*. It says "when the *yogī* remains inwardly attentive (*antar lakshya*), keeping the *chitta* (mind) and the *prāṇa* absorbed and sight steady, as if seeing everything while in reality seeing nothing outside, below, or above, verily it is called *Śāmbhavī mudrā* learned by favour of a *guru*. Whatever wonderful *śūnya* or *aśūnya* is perceived is to be regarded as the manifestation of the *Parama Śiva*".[30]

It says that when the *Brahma granthī* (in the heart) is pierced by the *Kuṇḍalinī* then a sort of delight is experienced in the vaccum of the heart, strange *anāhat* sounds are heard in the body, the *yogi*'s body becomes divine, glowing and his whole heart becomes void (*śūnya*).

In the second stage i.e. *Ghaṭāvasthā*, the airs (*Prāṇa* and *Apāna vāyu*) unite into one and begin to flow in the middle channel, the *Vishṇu granthi* is pierced resulting in feeling of highest pleasure and the *bherī* sound (like the beating of a Kettledrum) arises in the *Atiśunya* (vaccum in the throat). In the third i.e. *Parichayāvasthā*, sound of *mardal* is known to arise in the *śūnya* between the eyebrows and then the *vāyu* goes to the *Mahaśunya* and the state of *Sahajānanda* is reached.

In the fourth or *Nishpatti state*, which comes when the *Rudra-granthi* is pierced, and the *anil* (air) enters the seat of the Lord (*Śivapīṭha*), pleasant sound like that of flute is produced. The absorption of *chitta* or mind in this sound is called *Rāja-yoga* which results in perpetual feeling of

---

[29] *HYP*, IV, 64-67.

[30] *Ibid.*, IV. 68-100.

delight. *HYP* says that those who are ignorant of *Rāja-yoga* and practice only *Haṭha-yoga* waste their energy fruitlessly. The absorption (*laya*) produced by *nāda* gives rise to *unmanī* state. By practice, the mind becomes steady in the *nāda* and is absorbed in it. So long as the sounds continue to be heard there is consciousness of *ākāśa*, when the sounds disappear, then it is called (realisation of) Para-Brahman Paramātmā. Whatever is heard in the form of *nāda*, says *HYP*, is the *Śakti*, that which is formless (*nirākāra*); the final state of the *tattvas* is the Parameśvara.[31]

The above account in the *HYP* of the four stages of *yoga* mentioned by Gorakshanātha, leading to the absorption of *chitta* in the *nāda* and thus attaining *Rāja-yoga*, and its importance for those practicising *Haṭha-yoga,* shows that *Haṭha-yoga* is only a means for attaining the *Rāja-yoga*. This should remove considerable confusion about the nature and object of *Haṭha-yoga* and its relation with the *Rāja-yoga*.

As a result of *Yoga-sādhanā*, says Gorakshanātha and after acquiring *piṇḍa-siddhi*, one realises *Paramapada* which in view of the *Mahāsiddhas* is Śiva with *chidrūpa Śakti* inhering in Him. One should then experience complete identity between *Jivātmā* and *Parama Śiva*. *Jīva*'s real nature, he says, is manifested in four stages — *Sahaja, Saṃyama, Sopāya* and *Advaita*.[32]

Sahaja Jñāna: Although the Supreme Being (Parameśvara) in His *Viśvarūpa* is without any form or attributes (*nīrākāra, nirguṇa*), He manifests along with *Māyā* as this phenomenal universe. Having awareness of this truth that in reality there is no difference between the *Jivātmā* and the Paramātmān (Supreme Being), that the two are non-different, the adept experiences oneness with the Universal Supreme Soul.

---

[31] *Ibid.*

[32] *Siddha-Siddhānta-Paddhati*, V, 25.

The knowledge of this reality is *Sahaja-jñāna*, says Gorakshanātha.[33]

The knowledge or consciousness of one's true nature, the real Self, as being self-shining undivided Soul, in essence the Supreme Spirit, and inhering such consciousness in his true Self is *Sopāya-Jñāna*. Such constant awareness of one's real nature that one's true Self is not different from the Supreme Reality is *Sopāya*, and the non-dual form of the Supreme Reality is *Paramapada*. The Siddhās, says Goraksha, ever remain established in *Ātmasvarūpa Paramapada*. The awareness of complete non-difference between the *Jivātmā* and the Paramātman is *Sahaja-Jñāna* and to restrain the senses and *manas* by non-attachment and directing them towards the true nature of *ātmā* is *Saṃyama*, says Gorakshanātha.[34] This is similar to what Patañjali says about *Saṃyama*. By directing the mind to any particular object and fixing it there for a long time "separating the object from the internal part i.e. the form of thing vanishes and only its meaning remains in the mind". Here the 'meaning' is the true nature of the *ātman*.[35] As Kshemarāja in his Commentary on *Śiva Sūtras* says, *ātmā* is Universal Consciousness. Its *jñāna* means its realisation.[36] The non-difference between the *Jivātmā* and the Paramātmā has been thus emphasised by Gorakshanātha in *Gorakhabānī*. He says that *ātmā* is the most exalted God, He is *Guru*, He is the *Parama-tattva Śiva*, ..."[37] And *Gheranḍa Saṃhitā* says that the *ātmā* though confined in the body is *chaitanya*, eternal, the highest (*parama*).[38]

Importance of *Sadguru* for an adept or *Sadguru sevana*:

In *Siddha-Yogī-Sampradāya*, great importance is attached

---

[33] *Ibid.*, V. 26.

[34] *Ibid.*, V. 27-28.

[35] Patañjali's *Yoga-Sūtra*, III.4-5; Vivekānand, *Rāja-Yoga*, p.219.

[36] *Śiva-Sūtras*, p.192.

[37] *Gorakhabānī*, pp.94-95.

[38] *Gheranḍa Saṃhitā*, VII.20.

to a true and Self-realised enlightened religious preceptor, a *sadguru*. This is in consonance with the tradition in the field of Indian Philosophy and religion "characterised by a unanimous emphasis on *Gurū-vāda* or the doctrine of preceptor", Explaining this common feature, Shashibhushan Das Gupta says ".... in a sense all the systems of Indian Philosophy and religion are mystic, — for according to all the systems truth always transcends intellectual apprehension or discursive speculation, — it is to be intuited within through the help of the preceptor, who has already realised it. Truth is transmitted from the preceptor to the disciple, just as light from one lamp to the other. The only way of knowing the truth is, therefore, to seek the grace of the *Guru,* who, and who alone, can make one realise the Supreme Reality".[39] According to *Siddha-Siddhānta-Paddhati*, one can acquire the knowledge of realising the *Paramapada* only by listening to the *sadupadeśa* (preaching) and receiving instructions from a *sadguru* and carrying them out carefully and devotedly.[40] As *Śiva-Sūtras* say, "The *Guru* who has attained Self-realisation can alone help the aspirant in acquiring it".[41] It is only by his grace and *upadeśa*, says *Siddha-Siddhānta-Paddhati*, that a *yogī* becomes a *Siddha* and acquires all the *siddhis* (occult powers), the *yogī* then becomes all knowing, free from all doubts, and master of the occult powers. Without the *guru*'s grace, says *Siddha-Siddhānta-Paddhati*, all this is not possible even though one may have studied all the *Śāstrās*, or acquired the knowledge of the sciences, or he may have mastered the four *Vedas,* or he may be an assiduous student of *Vedānta*, or he may be knowledgeable about *ātma-tattva,* or he may be a good logician, or he may have even experienced the non-difference between *Jīvātmā* and

[39] *Obscure Religious Cults*, pp.87-88.
[40] *SSP*, V.31.
[41] *Śiva-Sūtras*, II.6.

Paramātmā, or he may have acquired *siddhi* in *Ajapā Gāyatrī mantra,* or may have meditated for long or performed *Japa* for long hours. He lays so much importance on the need of a *Sadguru* that he regards listening to his teachings and instructions as the only way to realise *Paramapada.* Neither by following the directions laid down in the *Śāstras*, nor by observing the rules and restrictions prescribed for the *Varṇas*, nor by solemn vows and *saṃkalpas*, nor by *aśaucha*, nor by offering libations to the Gods and the departed members of the family, nor by performing birth and death *saṃskāras* and rituals, nor by practising in a proper manner *Yoga, Āsana, Prāṇāyāma*, nor by non-attachment or *Vairāgya*, nor by observing *maun* or silence, nor by wearing *mudrās*, nor by observing food restrictions, nor by keeping fasts, nor by self-controlling the body, nor by praying one's deity, nor by following the *āshrama dharma*, nor by *japa* (repetition of God's name), nor by *tapa, dhyāna* (meditatin), *Yajñā*, nor by the knowledge of the six schools of Philosophy, nor by keeping *Jaṭā*, nor by shaving one's head, nor by visit to the *tīrthas* (holy places), nor by so many other ways can one realise *Paramapada*, as all these (ways) are realisable through the body. A Siddha Purusha, says Gorakshanātha, instead of taking recourse to these methods, remains established in *Ātma-svarūpa Paramapada.*[42]

In the aforesaid observations, Shrī Gorakshanātha, while following the poetic tradition of those times emphasises what really matters i.e. to abide identified with the Supreme Consciousness rather than depending on various other external supports and formal rules and regulations of religions.

Gorakshanātha goes on in this manner to emphasise the great importance and spiritual need of a *Sadguru* and describes at length how an adept moves from one stage to

---

[42] *SSP*, V, vss.31-35, 57-62.

another to acquire perfection during a period of twelve years of discipleship. Thus in the eleventh year he becomes all knowing and in the twelfth year, the *Yoga-Siddha Purusha* becomes like Śiva himself "venerated like Bhairava in all the three *lokas*", says Gorakshanātha.[43]

A *yoga sādhaka* (adept) desirous of acquiring inner peace should (therefore) seek refuge at the feet of a *Sadguru*, then the realisation of *Sāmarasya* and *Paramapada* easily come to him, and he attains *Pinḍa-siddhi* i.e. he realises the presence of *Para-Pinḍa* in his own physical body (*Vyashṭi-Pinḍa*).[44]

Who can be regarded a *Sadguru*? *Siddha-Siddhānta-Paddhati* says that an adept should receive instructions from a *Mahāsiddha Sadguru*. A *Mahāsiddha Yogī* or *Siddhapurusha* is one who has a deep insight into the five states of consciousness: *sthūla, sūkshma, kāraṇa, turya* and *turyātīta*.[45] There are seven *bhūmikās* of *yoga*, the first five being preparatory stages involving initiation, study of *Upanishads* and *Yoga-Śastra*, performing *āsana, prāṇāyama*, and *meditation* on the *Ātma-svarūpa*, to feel oneness with the whole Cosmic creation, non-attachment towards the worldly matters, and to abide in the *Advaita-svarūpa*. *Svarūpānanda* or divine delightful experience of abiding in the Supreme Spirit is the sixth *bhūmikā* and the seventh is the attainment of *Turyātīta* or *Kaivalyāvasthā*. This is a state of absolute unity between the soul and the Supreme Consciousness. A *yogī* who well understands these *avasthās* is called a *Siddhapurusha, Yogīsvareśvara*.[46] A *Mahāsiddha Sadguru* is self-realised and spiritually so elevated that by his mere words or even by his compassionate glance he makes it possible for the adept to realise the *Paramapada*, verily Śiva, realisable by one's own experience.

---

[43] *Ibid.*, V, vss.36-44.

[44] *Ibid.*, V, vs.45.

[45] *Ibid.*, V, vs.55.

[46] *Bhāratī*, p.62.

The *Sadguru* imparts to the disciple the knowledge of realising the *Paramapada* and after establishing him in the state of *sāmrasya*, teaches his disciple to abide in Him. By inherence of the individual Self in the *Paramapada*, says Gorakshanātha, the adept himself becomes a *Mahā-Siddha* and acquires deep insight into the Highest Reality.[47] By his preaching or even by his compassionate glance, the *guru* destroys all the eight bonds of the aspirant viz., *jarā* (old age), *janma* (birth), *mṛityu* (death), *vyādhi* (sickness), *kāma* (longing), *krodha* (anger), *moha* (delusion, attachment), *avidyā* (primal ignorance), and *ahaṃkāra* (pride) and establishes him in the Divine bliss of the Supreme Being.[48]

Not only this, a *sadguru*, in a moment, by *Śaktipāta*,[49] or even by his mere compassionate glance, establishes his disciple in *Ātma-svarūpa Parampada*, says Goraksha.[50] By his words and teachings, the *sadguru* dispels the ignorance of the aspirant and enables him to cross the ocean of existence. By his kindly glance a *Sadguru* can liberate an aspirant of the worldly bonds.[51]

---

[47] *Siddha-Siddhānta-Paddhati*, IV, 56, 64-66. Cf. *Mālinīvijaya* which says that the "Absorption of the individual consciousness in the Divine results from an awakening imparted by the guru in one who has freed his mind of all ideation" (*Śiva-Sūtras*)

[48] *Ibid.*, V. 66-68.

[49] *SSP*, V.65. For a very exhaustive discussion on the meaning and nature of *Śaktipāta*, see M.M. Gopinath Kaviraj's *Tāntrika Sādhanā aur Siddhānta*, pp.78-98. It is described as a way of establishing oneself in *Ātma-svarūpa* and results from grace and rise of true knowledge. *Śaktipāta* can be broadly classified as of three types — *tīvra* (swift), *madhya* (middling) and *manda* (slow). Sometimes this knowledge comes from the *guru* or by the study of the *Śāstras*, but sometimes it emerges by itself like a flash. It is then called *Pratibha Jñāna* which is superior to *Jñāna* received from the *guru* or derived from the *Śāstras*. It is the *Mahā-Jñāna* and one automatically comes to understand the nature of *Jīva, Īśvara, Māyā* and other bonds. By *Pratibha-Jñāna* one becomes aware of the sway of Parameśvara, both inside and outside the body.

[50] *Siddha-Siddhānta-Paddhati*, V, 69.

[51] *Siddha-Siddhānta-Paddhati*, V, 70. The concept of 'liberation' in Kashmir Śaivism is very similar, i.e. "the recognition of ones true nature, the original, . . .

In brief, according to Gorakshanātha, without the grace of the *guru*, it is very difficult to reach the state of *viśrānti* achieved by annihilation of the *chitta-vṛittis*. In the state of *viśranti*, the *Samashṭi* and *Vyashti-pinḍa* are in an undifferentiated state i.e. in a state of *sāmarasya* and the adept is fully established in *Paramapada*.[52]

On attaining *chitta-viśrānti* i.e. cessation of *chitta-vṛittis*, it is easy for a yogī who is keen and firm in *yoga-sādhanā* to realise *nirutthāna*, in which state, the *Paramapada*, which is so difficult to realise, becomes manifest and the individual body becomes one with the Cosmic Body.[53]

. . . innate, pure I — consciousness ... when one has this awareness and one knows one's real nature, one is liberated", as Abhinavagupta (*Tantrā*, II, 192) says. But *moksha* or liberation i.e. awareness of one's true nature is not the highest attainment which is Śiva – consciousness when the entire universe appears as I or Śiva. (*Siva-Sūtras*, xxx).

[52] *SSP*, V, 81-83.

[53] *Ibid.*, V, 84. See also, Gopināth Kaviraj's *Tāntrika Sādhanā aur Siddhānta*, pp.391-92.

Chapter VIII

Avadhūta

Gorakhanātha in his sixth *Upadeśa* in *Siddha-Siddhānta-Paddhati* explains at length the attributes of an *Avadhūta*. He says that one can acquire *nitya-avadhūta-svarūpa* by establishing *sāmarasya* between the *Jīvātmā* and *Paramātmā*, between the *vyashṭi pinḍa* (individual body) and *Brahmāṇḍa* (Cosmic body).[1]

What is the *svarūpa* of an *Advadhūta-yogī*? *Siddha-Siddhānta-Paddhati* says that one who has removed the natural *vikāras* arising from the body, *jñānendriyas* or powers of sense-perception, mind and other worldly entanglements, and is steeped in *nirmatva svarūpa*, who has eliminated from his mind the pleasures of the senses and has withdrawn his mind from them, and thus getting rid of all dualistic conditions, remains engrossed in the meditation of the Supreme Consciousness (*Parama Śiva*), is an *Avadhūta yogī*.[2]

Goraksha-Siddhānta-Saṃgraha answers the question as to who can be called an *Avadhūta*? Whose every *vachana* (word) is (like) *Veda* i.e. full of *jñāna*, it says, whose feet are like a *tīrtha* (holy place) having the power to bring liberation, whose kind glance is (bestower of) *Kaivalya*, who shows others the path of welfare, who has in one hand renunciation and in the other worldly enjoyments i.e. by whose grace everything is obtainable, but who himself is untouched by both, who is free from all the defects of the natural *vikāras* — mental and physical.[3]

---

[1] *Siddha-Siddhānta-Paddhati* (*SSP*), VI.1.

[2] *Ibid.*

[3] *Goraksha-Siddhānta-Saṃgraha,* pp.2-3.

Going back to the *Siddha-Siddhānta-Paddhati*, it continues to dwell on the attributes of an *Avadhūta*, placing the highest ideals before an aspirant who wishes to reach this high level in the Nātha sect. It says that an *Avadhūta* is one who has destroyed by force or uprooted the web of the five afflictions viz., *avidyā* (primal ignorance), *asmitā* (egoism), *rāga* (intense desire), *dvesha* (envy) and *abhiniveśa* (too much adherence) and who has freed himself from the manifold diversities of *jāgrata, svapna* and *sushupti* (waking, dream and deep sleep) states.[4] He is firmly established in *ātma-svarūpa*,[5] (essential Self) and is free from determination and differences of perception.[6]

He wears only a *kaupīna* on his waist and has a *kharpara* (begging bowl) in his hand, says *Siddha-Siddhānta-Paddhati*, and he moves in the world with a countenance intended not to excite pity, but as one for whom nothing is beyond his power or accomplishment, and who is entirely without fear.[7]

Gorakhanātha further says that the ashes smeared on the body of an *Avadhūta* symbolise his having reduced to ash the aforesaid five afflictions (*avidya, asmitā*, etc.), the *Śaṅkha* (conch-shell) in his hand is a combination of two letters — '*śaṅ*' which is expressive of contentment and happiness and the letter '*kha*' is expressive of Para-Brahman. Establishing

---

[4] In *svapna* or dream state only *prāṇa* and *manas* are active. The eyes, ear, touch, etc. are not active, their functions being taken over by *manas* or mind. In *sushupti* state i.e. in the state of profound sleep, function of *manas* also stops, only *prāṇa* functions.

[5] The expression "*ātma-svarūpa*" frequently occurs in *Siddha-Siddhānta-Paddhati*. This may be clear from *Śiva Saṃhitā*, II.53-54 which says "when a person does not see anything else here having seen the Self by the Self then there is no sin in renouncing all *karma*. All the desires and the rest are dissolved through Gnosis only. When all (minor) *tattvas* (principles) cease to exist then *svayam tattva* becomes manifest". Divine Self or *ātma svarūpa* conveys the same sense.

[6] *SSP*, VI. vss.3-5.

[7] *Ibid.*, VI, vs.5; *Bhāratī*, II.p.5.

himself in *ātma-svarūpa*, an *Avadhūta* by his teachings and *yoga-sādhanā* tries to keep others on the right path, thus contributing to their well-being.[8]

All what an *Avadhūta* wears or keeps with him have some meaningful symbolism or the other, says Goraksha. The *padukās* on his feet are symbolic of his knowledge of the Supreme Spirit, the deer skin which he carries with him indicates that he is adorned by *anāhata-nāda*, the *Śelī* on his head-dress symbolises *parā-saṃvita* or the Supreme Consciousness, and the *mekhalā* round his waist indicates *nivṛitti* or detachment (*vairāgya*) from worldly activities,[9] His firm *āsana* suggests that he is firmly established in *ātma-svarūpa*. He further says that an *Avadhūta* is free from *kāma* (longing), *krodha* (anger), *lobha* (greed), *moha* (attachment), *mada* (pride), *matsara* (envious disposition) and other *vikāras* (deviation from the natural, mental or physical state). The pair of *kuṇḍala* (rings) in his ears suggest that he is endowed with *chitprakāśa* or light of the Supreme Consciousness and *paramānanda* (supreme bliss), his *japamālā* or rosary is symbolic of a mind dwelling in complete peace. The *daṇḍa* or stick which he carries in his hand is suggestive of patience, the *kharpara* or begging bowl which he carries is like *parākāśa*, limitless in space, and his *yogapaṭṭa* is like *Nijā-Śakti*. One who is adorned with these qualities and attainments is an *Avadhūta*, says Gorakshanātha.[10] Here *Siddha-Siddhānta-Paddhati* has mentioned most of the *vesha-pratīka* or

---

[8] *Ibid.*, VI, vs.6.

[9] *SSP*, VI. vss.7-8; There are four kinds of *vairāgya* or detachment from worldly matters: *Mṛidu* (intermittent, weak), *Madhyama* (middling), *Adhimātra* (high degree when worldly enjoyments even become a source of pain) and *Para* (where mind turns away from the worldly matters to an extent that it cannot be brought back under any circumstances). "Corresponding to the four *Yogas*, the mildest form of *vairāgya* being the mark of the *Mantra-Yoga* and the greatest degree of detachment being the mark of the *Rāja-Yoga*". *The Six Centres and the Serpent Power*, p.255 n.3).

[10] *SSP*, VI, vss.7-10.

distinctive marks of a Nātha Yogī, and their inner meaning. Gorakhsha always emphasises the inner meaning or feeling as being far more important than externalities.

Not only this, an *Avadhūta* is one, continues Gorakha, who is above *bhedā-bheda* (difference and the identity of God and the Universe), *dvaïta-advaita* (duality-non-duality)[11] and who is anxious to enjoy the bliss of self-realisable *akhaṇḍa* (undivided) *ātmarasa*, and is steeped in Sachchidānanda *svarūpa*, who realises in his own self the all pervading Paramātman (the Supreme Spirit, who is above the limits of space and time), and who has tasted the nectar from the moon which flows down from the *Sahasrāra*. He has cleared his *Vajranāḍī* of all impurities (by *Prāṇāyāma* etc.), has by *Vajrolī* turned upward the flow of *vīrya* (semen) bringing it under control and has realised in his own self the non-difference between *ātmā* (individual Soul) and Paramātman (Supreme Soul), and by achieving *sāmarasya* is established in *Ātma-pada*.[12]

Gorakshanātha lays down, as mentioned earlier, the most exacting requirements for being considered an *Avadhūta*. He further says that an *Avadhūta* is one who has realised in himself the undivided Supreme Spirit and is established there, is fully absorbed in the feeling of *anutthāna* in which state nothing arises in the mind and there is complete dissolution of the mind. In that state he experiences oneness of *ātmā* and Paramātmā, and is contentedly established in *Sachchidānanda Parama-tattva*. He is an *Avadhūta* who reveals (to others) the true nature of the *avyakta* (non-manifest) Paramātmā residing within them. He illuminates the world by the light of his knowledge, and experiences divine bliss in the

---

[11] The *dvaittavādina* assert the two principles or existence of human soul as separate from the Supreme Being whereas *advaitavādin* assert identity of Bramhan or of the Paramātman or Supreme Soul with *Jīvātmā* or human soul.

[12] *SSP*, VI, vss.11-15.

undivided (sole) Divine light, and his approach towards everyone is correct and healthy. He remains firmly established in *akhaṇḍa-svarūpa* (undivided real nature) in diverse roles of a *bhogī* (worldly person), *yogī*, *digambara*, *Yogīrāja, Guru*, in all characters in fact.[13] In this way, in *nitya prakāśa* i.e. pure, enlightened all pervading *ātma-svarūpa*, he demonstrates the true purport of diverse philosophies and principles. That *Yogī Avadhūta* is a *sadguru* because he has realised in himself the synthesis of all the different schools of philosophies. In everything, everywhere he sees his own true Self, says Goraksha.[14]

Gorakshanātha explains at length the last observation made above. He says that an *Avadhūta* is *atyāśramī* i.e. above the four stages of the *āśrama dharma* since he remains established in *akhaṇḍa ātma-svarūpa* which is within his own self.[15] He is like the God as he has power, and he is master of himself having acquired complete self-control. He is contented as he has attained his objective and he is virtuous and saintly. He (*Yogī Avadhūta*) is master of his senses, he is seeker of the Reality (*tattva-chintaka*), and seeks to understand and synthesise *Chāravāka, Arhata* (Jainism), *Bauddha, Nyāya, Vaiśeshika, Sāṃkhya, Mīmāṃsā* and various other schools of Philosophy, and since he fully knows the nature of the real Self, he is *sarvā-svarūpa Yogī*, (knowing) *Ātmā, Paramātmā, Jīvātmā, Svarūpa*, Śiva, Rudra, an Avadhūta Yogī is manifestly a *sarvātmā*, says *Siddha-Siddhānta-Paddhati*.[16]

Explaining further the above observation, Goraksha says that in every living thing exists *padma kuhere* (*ātma-svarūpa*) which dwells in the heart. Everyone desirous of attaining

---

[13] *Ibid.*, VI, vss.16-19.

[14] *Ibid.*, VI, vs.20.

[15] *Ibid.*, VI, vs.21.

[16] *Ibid.*, VI, vss.21-24.

moksha should free it from the various bonds, such as attachment, sorrow, etc., and establish oneself in *akhaṇḍa ātma-svarūpa*. This *ātma svarūpa* or *ātma-tattva*, he says, is verily Brahmā, Vishṇu, Rudra, *Akshara* (name of Brahma), Svaraṭ, Indra, *Prāṇa, Kāla, Agni, Chandramā* (Moon), *Sūrya* (Sun) and *Parama Śiva*. By practicing *Yoga*, one experiences or realises the self-realisable *tattva*.[17]

Those who follow and understand *Sāṃkhya*, says Gorakshanātha further, know Him as *Parama Purusha*. The *Pūrva-mīmāṃsakas* performing various *yajñas* also see the Supreme Reality as such. The *Vedas* and *Vedānta Sūtras* call Him as *Paramānanda Svarūpa Paramātmā*. In this way He is described in different philosophical schools differently, though He is not different. He is the bestower of happiness and His *ātma-tattva* is the Supreme Truth of the oneness and identity of *Jīvātmā* and Paramātmā, says Gorakshanātha. An *Avadhūta yogī*, in the light of his knowledge of *Yoga* gathers the true nature of Self and abides in the indivisible *ātma-svarūpa* enlightening the *ātma-tattva*.[18]

Though an *Avadhūta yogī* is not bound by the rules and regulations of the *āśrama* system, he is in reality a *Brahmachārī* since he is a *Brahma jñānī* and self-realised, says Gorakshanātha. Though immersed in Supreme Consciousness and *yoga sādhanā*, an *Avadhūta* is a *Gṛihastha* (householder) too as undivided Brahmarūpatva is his life-companion and all pervading *śunya* (*vyoma* or sky) is his home. He is also a *Vānaprastha*, says Goraksha, since after eliminating the thought constructs or *chitta-vṛittis*, he meditates solely on Brahman in the solitude of a forest like *akhaṇḍa antarjyoti* (light of the Self). In fact, expressing his views against all external practices, rituals and superficial aspects, he says that one does not become a *Vānaprastha* simply by dwelling in a forest like a deer.[19]

---

[17] *Ibid.*, VI, vss.25-27.
[18] *Ibid.*, VI, vss.28-33.
[19] *Ibid.*, VI, vss.34-36.

Taking the analogy further, he says that an *Avadhūta yogī* who sees no difference between *Jivātmā* and *Paramātmā* is a *Sanyāsī* as he lays aside all his *saṃkalpas* (determinations and desires) and concentrates on the Divine Reality, the soul. A *Yogī Avadhūta* is like a *Trdanḍī Sanyāsī*, says Gorakshanātha, as by his knowledge of the *tattva-jñāna* he frees himself from the bonds of *Māyā* (*avidyā, karma, kalājāla* etc.) and becomes firmly established in Supreme Consciousness (*akhaṇḍa ātma-svarūpa*). One does not become a *Tridanḍī Sanyāsī*, he says, by merely carrying three bamboo sticks. A *yogī Avadhūta* is an *Ekadanḍī Sanyāsī*, as he controls his *chitta* or empirical mind, which is so unsteady due to the habitual tendencies of the mind, arising from various *vikāras, vṛittis, saṃkalpa-vikalpa* etc.[20]

An *Avadhūta yogī* is a Śaiva, says Gorakshanātha, as he realises the Reality, pure, formless, *Paramānanda svarūpa*, self-luminous *Parameśvara* (Śiva). That yogī is a *Tapasvī* too as by controlling the sense organs, which are naturally attracted towards the pleasures of the senses, he merges them in *akhaṇḍa ātma svarūpa* or Divine Self.[21] And he is a *Pāśupata* (*Śaiva*) also, continues the great *Yogī*, as he gives up *paśutva* or tendencies of brutality and beastiality, and preparing himself for the worship of the *akhaṇḍa Parātpara Parama Śiva*, establishes himself in *Śiva-rūpa*. He is a *Kālamukha* too as he worships the *Liṅga*, which is *Sachchidānanda svarūpa*, the cause of this creation, and is ever present in His *pīṭha*. He is a *Vīra Śaiva Liṅgadhārī* as he bravely overcomes the attitude of pride towards all living beings. He (*Avadhūta*) is a *Digambara Nirvāṇī Sanyāsī* as he renounces the worldly things and is free from any veil over pure Consciousness. And he is in reality a *Kāpālika* too as after receiving the *mantra* from the *Guru*, he follows the

---

[20] *Ibid.*, VI, vss.37-39.

[21] *Ibid.*, VI, vss.40-41.

sādha mārga as directed by the *Guru* and remains fully established in *Śiva-svarūpa*, and meditates only on his *upāsya* (one to be revered or worshipped). One who knows the *Mahākāraṇa Śakti*, the unity of *Kula* and *Akula*, and is a worshipper of *Śakti* is a *Śākta*, says Goraksha. One who knows (reverently) *Śakti Mahākālī*, in whom all the *kalās* merge is a *Śākta jñānī*. By understanding the *Kula-Akula* Reality in a proper order, who perceives unity in the same order and is established in *Śakti-pada* is a Śākta, says Goraksha.[22]

Gorakshanātha further dwells on the attributes of a *Śākta*. He says that one who gives up the five *makāras*, viz., *madya, mudrā, mīna*, *pala* (*māns*) and *maithuna* is a *Śākta*. *Siddha-Siddhānta-Paddhati* says that here *madya* means *mada* or pride, *mudrā* means craving for fulfilment of one's desires, *mīna* (fish) is *māyā*, *pala* (meat, *māns*) is (difficult to control) *mana*, and *maithuna* means union of *prāṇa* and *apāna*. One who has surrendered or given up these five *makāras* at the feet of the *Mahā-śakti* is called a *Śākta*, says Goraksha. One who understands or follows these *pañcha-makāra* in this (*sātvika*) sense, is indeed a *Śākta*.[23]

Further, says Gorakshanātha, a *Śākta* is one who knows that *Śakti* by Her own unique power impels the creation of *Jagat* (world process) characterised by light, motion and action, and is in fact the expression of *Brahma-rūpa*, and who in the state of *nirvyuthāna*, establishes himself in *akhaṇḍa Sachchidānanda rūpa*.[24]

---

[22] *Ibid.*, VI, vss.42-49.

[23] *Ibid.*, VI, vs.50. What name can be given to a language, when the intention is to convey something different from what is expressed by the words? P.C. Bagchi (*Studies in the Tantra*, p.27), like Vidushekhar Shastri does not name it as "*Sāndhā-bhāshā* or twilight *bhāsha*, as M.M. H.P. Shastri does, but as "*abhiprāyika vachana* i.e. intentional speech", and says that literal interpretation of some terms and verses, such as in many Vajrayānī works "can lead one into worst morality".

[24] *SSP*, VI, vss.51-52.

An *Avadhūta yogī* is a *Vaishṇava* too, says *Siddha-Siddhānta-Paddhati*, as he knows that *Vishṇupada Alakha Nirañjana tattva*, which is pervading the whole universe dwells in his own individual body (*vyashṭi-pinḍa*) and is manifested in an undifferentiated manner.[25] And he is also a *Bhāgavata* as he experiences in his own individual body the all pervading self-illumined totally undifferentiated *Bhāgavata-tattva*. He has knowledge of *Pañcharātra* i.e. the knowledge of the dissolution of the Universe and disappearance of the gross form of the five physical elements, and so *Avadhūta* is *Pañcharātrika* also. He is also a *Sātvika* since he has a loving adoration for the Supreme Reality, the Universal Soul and he reposes all his actions arising from his sense organs in Him, and in his effort to attain *mukti*, his mind is ever engrossed in self-illumined, all knowing Consciousness. And he is a Kshapaṇava also as after uprooting *rāga-dvesha* (attachment-hatred), he controls his *chitta-vṛittis* (thought constructs) and is naked like the sky.[26]

In this way Gorakshanātha has described not only the qualities and attainments an *Avadhūta* should have but also that he should not hesitate to learn even from a *Kshapaṇava* knowing the *abhiprāyaka vachana* or meaning of the characteristics associated with him, and to feel one with every class of people, and to have hatred for none.

Śakti creates the *sṛishṭi* (universe) says Gorakshanātha, and She is absorbed in Śiva at the time of *pralaya* or dissolution. One who strengthens the notion of the union or non-difference between *Śiva* and *Śakti* is a *Siddha Yogirāja*. In the state of *nirvikalpa samādhi* when all *chitta-vṛittis* have disappeared, he feels one with the Supreme Reality. He is

---

[25] Cf. *Śiva-Sūtras*, I.16 "when the aspirant becomes aware of the universe as Śiva, then he becomes like Sadā Śiva, free from limited self". *Śiva-Sūtras*, I.16. p.62.

[26] *SSP*, VI, vss.53-63.

indeed a *Mahāyogī* who has dissolved all his *vṛittis* in his soul, who rids himself of all pleasures of the senses, is ever free from passions and establishes himself in his *sva-svarūpa* or true Self, manifesting his *chaitanya-rūpa* and is wholly established in *Sachchidānanda*.[27] He is of the nature of indivisible Consciousness, above all dualities, free from *vikāras* and is ever cheerful. He has no desire or craving for wealth and does not grieve on its loss or destruction. In fact he feels happy in the absence of worldly things and is absorbed in supreme bliss of self-realisable Reality. He is not scared of death or destruction.[28]

In this way, that *Avadhūta Sadguru* is worthy of praise who brings 'realisation of synthesis' of all schools of thought and principles in the same *Para-Brahma Sachchidānanda*. By synthesising the views of all the different schools of philosophy, says Gorakshanātha, the state of *viśrānti* is achieved, and the *yogī* is absorbed in *Para-Brahman Parameśvara*. He becomes *Brahma svarūpa*. A *Brahman svarūpa yogī* is worthy of reverence, he says.[29]

One should take refuge in *Siddha-Siddhānta-mata*, says Gorakshanātha. The *Vedāntists* renouncing *karmopāsnā* (worship involving ceremonial acts and sacrifices) enter into disputation on the question of duality and non-duality and praise *advaita* as the (only) true course, and loose sight of the thought behind the concept. *Pūrva-Mīmāṃsaka*, the followers of Sāṃkhya philosophy, *Vaishṇava, Vīra Śaiva, Bauddha, Jain, Yogīs, Maunavratadhārīs, Śunyavādīs, Vairāgīs*, those who have succeeded in making *Kuṇḍalinī* rise up to the *Sahasrāra* and then return to the *Mūlādhāra*, those who have mastered the *Kheecharī mudrā* etc. remain deprived from the realisation of their *sat-svarūpa* (true Self). Hence, he says,

[27] *Ibid.*, VI.63-67.
[28] *Ibid.*, VI, vss.66-68.
[29] *Ibid.*, VI, vss.69-70.

one should take refuge in the *Siddha-Siddhānta-mata* in which by *samraskaraṇa*, in the state of *viśrānti* (which comes on the cessation of all *vikalpas)*, one realises the *abhedatā* (non-difference) between the *Jīvātmā* (the individual soul) and the Paramātmā (Supreme Soul). Without *samarasakaraṇa* (absorption in the Supreme Consciousness which continues even when one is not engaged in formal meditation) one cannot realise *Paramapada* which is of the form of *niryutthāna*. By taking recourse to others means one achieves only partial self-realisation (*ātma-bodha*) and is unable to realise *Paramapada*, the eternal, omnipresent, *nirpeksha-svarūpa Alakha Nirañjana*, attainable with the help of the *jñāna* imparted by a *Guru*.[30]

Siddha-Siddhānta-Paddhati says that by experiencing the true Self, an *Avadhūta yogī* synthesises all schools of philosophies. In the context of the synthetic approach towards different schools of Philosophies advocated by Gorakshanātha, Brahma's observations about the Tāntrism as a whole are relevant. He writes, "The philosophy of the Tantras which is a reconciliation of the absolute monism of the *Upanishads* and the dualism or qualified monism preached by the *Purāṇas*, and the Tāntric method of *sādhanā*, which combines in it *yoga* and *Bhakti*, *mantra* and *homa* (oblations), *jñāna* and *karma* prove beyond doubt that the Tāntrism can be best studied as the synthesis of all that was good in the various forms of (Hindu) *sādhanā*".

---

[30] *Ibid.*, VI, vss.73-93; *Philosophy of Hindu Sādhanā*, p.275.

Chapter IX

Goraksha-Śataka, Haṭha-Yoga and Some important concepts of the Nātha Philosophy

The sources which inform us about the philosophy and *yogic* practices of the Nātha Sampradāya can be broadly divided into two categories: those which mainly contain exposition of the metaphysical concepts of the Nāthas. such as *Kaula-Jñāna-Nirṇaya*, *Siddha-Siddhānta-Paddhati*, *Goraksha-Siddhānta-Saṃgraha*, *Amaraugh-aprabodha*, *Jñāna-Kārikā,* etc., and those which discuss mainly the *yogic* practices in the *Haṭha* system of *yoga*, such as *Goraksha-Śataka, Yoga-vishaya, Yogamārtanḍagrantha, Haṭha-Yoga-Pradīpikā, Gheranḍa Saṃhitā* and many others works. At the same time, many of these works defy any strict categorisation and even in the works of the latter category, the philosophy of the sect finds ample expression. As we will see in this Chapter, without first knowing the philosophical concepts of the Nātha sect, one can gain only an inadequate understanding of the Haṭha manuals and the practices described therein. In fact one of the main aims of this brief chapter is to understand *Goraksha-Śataka*, believed to have been composed by Gorakshanātha himself in the 12th century i.e. much earlier than *Haṭha-Yoga-Pradīpikā*, which is assigned to the 15th century, and *Gheranḍa Saṃhitā* which is even a later work, in the context of the Nātha philosophy. At times, it may even appear that we are using *Goraksha-Śataka,* which is in itself a very important text, as a peg to delineate further the philosophy of this sect already discussed in the preceding chapters, as it is not much known, especially among the educated classes, as observed by M.M. Gopinatha Kaviraja long back in 1923, in a paper '*Chakras* according to Gorakshanātha' (*Saraswati Bhavan Series*, Vol.II, 1923).

The very first line of the work, preceding the first verse says, "*Oṁ, Haṭha-yoga Gorakshaśataka prārambhaḥ*" making it clear that it is a work on *Haṭha-Yoga*. Later, towards the end of the work, Gorakshanātha devotes a number of verses on the importance of and benefits from repeating the sacred word '*Oṁ*'. Sitting in *Padmāsana* (Lotus Posture), he says, holding the body and neck steady, fixing the sight on the tip of the nose, repeat the word '*Oṁ*' in which the three *lokas* viz. *Bhūr, Bhuvar* and *Svar* and the divinities Soma (Moon), Sūrya (Sun) and the *Agni* (fire) exist. In '*Oṁ*', the three *kālas* (past, present and future), the three *Vedas*, the three *svaras*, the three *devas* (*trayodeva*) reside. '*Oṁ*', he says, is the supreme light (*parama jyoti*) and contains *kriyā* (action), *ichchā* (desire), *jñāna* (knowledge) and the three *Śaktis* viz. Brāhmī, Raudrī and Vaishṇavī. He says, "With voice repeat that *Bījam* (i.e. '*Oṁ*'), practice it with the body (i.e. using postures), and with the mind (*manasa*), remember it (i.e. mediate on '*Oṁ*') which is *parama jyoti* (i.e. supreme light), and one who recites the *Praṇava* i.e. '*Oṁ*' continually is not besmirched by sin as the leaf of the lotus flower is not touched by water.[1]

The importance attached to this sacred word, '*Oṁ*' among the Nāthas can be judged from the fact that in *Gorakhabodha*, which is in the form of a long interlocution between Gorāksha and his Guru, Matsyendra, Goraksha invariably begins with the words '*Oṁ Gurujī*'.[2] The *ārtīs*, *mantras* and *stutis* of the Nāthas also begin with this word of profound religious

[1] *Goraksha-Śataka* (*GŚ*), vss.83-89; *Dhyāna-bindu Upanishad* (in *Thirty Minor Upanishads*, tr. Narayanasvami Aiyar), p.202.

[2] *Nātha Sampradāya aur Sūkshma Veda* (*NSSV*), pp.64-88.

efficacy and object of meditation and veneration.[3] In *Jñānatilaka* also, Gorakshanātha says that by meditating on *Praṇava* i.e. '*Oṁ*', one can realise *Para-Brahma* (Supreme Spirit) which is omnipresent and eternal (*avināśī*).[4] In *Shaṭ-Chakra-Nirūpaṇa,* a part of *Śri-Tattva-Chintāmaṇi* by Pūrṇānanda Yati, '*Oṁ*; is described as the first *bīja* of the *Vedas*.[5] The eternal *bīja*, says *Śiva-Saṃhitā,* is in the two petalled *Ājñā Chakra*, situated between the eye-brows, brilliant as the autumnal moon. This is the great light and by meditating on this, one attains the highest success.[6] *Śivopanishad* says that *Praṇava* (*Oṁ*) is the life-giving force of all the *Prāṇas* and enshrines in itself the *Vedas*, Deva, *yoni*, *dhyeya* (final object) and to meditate on '*Oṁ*' even for a moment will result in the same benedictions as performance of one-thousand *yajñās*. Patañjali says (I.27), that '*Oṁ*' is the manifesting word of *Īśvara,* the *Purusha Vishesha*. Commenting on this *sūtra* and the following few *sūtras* Vivekanand says, "Around this word '*Oṁ*' are centred all the different religious ideas in India; all the various religious ideas of the *Vedas* have gathered themselves round the word '*Oṁ*' .... The word has been retained at every stage of the religious growth in India and has been manifested to mean all the various ideas about God."[7] *Sūtras* 28-29 say that "by repetition of '*Oṁ*' and by meditating upon its meaning one gains knowledge of introspection, and mental and physical obstacles (diseases, bodily ailments, doubts, *pramāda*, grief, non-retention of concentration etc.) are removed".[8] *Śiva-Śaṃhitā* says that when a *yogī*, after piercing the six *chakras* reaches the *parichaya* state in which the air leaving the right and left nostril remain unmoved in the *Sushumnā*, he should

---

[3] *Ibid.*, pp.160-66.

[4] *Jñānatilaka*, p.207 in *Gorkhabāni* (ed. Dr. Badathvāla).

[5] *Śri-tattva-chintāmaṇi* (*Shaṭ-chakra-nirūpaṇa*), vs.33.

[6] *Śiva Saṃhitā*, V, vss.97-98.

[7] Patañjali, *Yoga-Sūtra*, I.24-28; *Rāja-Yoga*, pp.141-45.

[8] *Ibid.*. I.28-29.

destroy all the *karmas* (cause of birth and death) by repetition of *Praṇava* (*Oṁ*) and should accomplish *kāya-vyūha* so that he may bear the consequences of all his accumulated *karmas* in one life without needing a re-birth.[9]

As to the importance of the work *Goraksha-śataka*, the author says that what he is describing is supreme knowledge which brings supreme bliss (*parama-ānanda*) and one can realise the *Paramapada,* and that it is like a ladder to the final release (*mukti*). Also, by its knowledge, mind is turned away from the sensual enjoyments and is attached to the Paramātmā.[10]

The last lines of the above para at least show that the criticism of *Haṭha-Yoga* as being more concerned with the body and not being a spiritual discipline is ill-founded. As Goraksha himself says, *Haṭha-Yoga* is only a means to attain the much higher objectives viz., *parama ānanda, Paramapada* and *mukti* etc., terms which have been discussed earlier.

We have already discussed the relation between *Haṭha-yoga* and *Rāja-yoga.* As noted, *Ghranḍa Saṃhitā* describes *Haṭha-yoga* "as the first rung of the ladder that leads to *Rāja-yoga*" and *Haṭha-Yoga Pradīpikā* says (IV.102) that "All the methods (*upāya*) of *Haṭha-yoga* are meant for gaining success in *Rāja-yoga*".[11] *Śiva-Saṃhitā* also lays emphasis on the need to learn *Haṭha-yoga* before proceeding further towards *Rāja-yoga*[12] in which the highest aim is *mukti* from Prakṛiti (*Māyā* of the *Advaitavādis*)". As Mikel Burley, criticising the idea that "*Haṭha-Yoga* incorporates only the 'lower' or 'physical' elements of the *yoga*" says that "*Haṭha* is a distinct tradition within the broader field of Indian soteriology that places a strong emphasis upon the integrity of physical, subtle-

---

[9] *Śiva-Saṃhitā*, III, 61-62.

[10] *GŚ*, vss.3-6.

[11] *Gheranḍa Saṃhitā*, p.1; *Haṭha-Yoga-Pradīpikā*, IV, 102.

[12] *Śiva-Saṃhitā*, V, 181.

physical and mental discipline for the attainment of the very highest goal – *Rāja-yoga* or *kaivalya* of the *Yoga-Sūtra*".[13]

At the outset it may be mentioned that there is a great similarity in many concepts of Vajrayāni Siddhas, such as Sarahapāda, and the Nātha Siddhas, such as Matsyendra, Goraksha and others. Thus the great *Vajrayānī Siddha* Sarahapāda has thus described *Paramapada*. On realising it, the *Jīva* ever experiences highest bliss (*mahā-sukha*) and that *Paramapada* is beyond *dvaita* or *advaita* or *vishishṭādvaita*. There is no place for *bhāva* (worldly existence) or *nirvāṇa*. There is neither *nirati* nor *surati*, neither *yoga* nor *bhoga*, illness or death. Neither sun nor moon enter there; there is neither movement of *mana* nor of *pavana*, neither *vāṇī* nor *Oṁkāra* are there. It is a differenceless state in which nothing exists, having merged or absorbed in One viz., *Śuddha Nirañjana Brahma*. There, one always hears *Anāhata nāda*.[14] In *Sabada*, 110 in *Gorakhabānī*, we find almost an identical description of *Paramapada*.[15] As for '*mukti*', *Goraksha-siddhānta-Saṃgraha* defines it as attainment of *Nātha svarūpa*. What is *Nātha svarūpa*? To put it in the briefest form, the 'Nātha' combines both the aspects of the Supreme Spirit (which they designate Parama Śiva in the Nātha tradition) (1) *Nirguṇa* and (2) His transcendent Supreme Power, *Śakti*, innate or immanent in Him.[16]

In vs. 7 of *Goraksha-Śataka*, the author describes the six *aṅgas* of the *Haṭha-Yoga* viz. *āsana, prāṇāyāma, pratyāhāra, dhāraṇā, dhyāna* and *samādhi*. These terms have already been discussed in detail in Ch.V as well as the reason for

---

[13] Mikel Burley, *Haṭha-Yoga*, p.124.

[14] *Dohā Kośa*, No.49-51, p.13, No.82-83, p.20; Dvijram Yadava, *Sarahapāda*, p.174; For similarity between *Siddha mārga* or *Haṭha-mārga* and *Vajra* or *Sahaja-mārga*, Gopinath Kaviraj's *Bhārtīya Sādhanā kī dhārā*, p.97.

[15] *Gorakhabānī, Sabad*, 110-111 (pp.38-39).

[16] *Goraksha-Siddhānta-Saṃgraha*, p.1.

omission to mention *Yama* and *Niyama*. In *Yoga Mārtanḍa*, Gorakshanātha describes *Samādhi* as that state in which the individual soul is completely merged in the *parama-jyoti* of the Absolute Spirit and closing all outlets of *prāṇa*, one should try to see that transcendental luminosity.[17] As noted earlier, in the state of *Samādhi*, there is total absorption of the self-consciousness in the Supreme Consciousness or Supreme Spirit and there is no duality between the *kartā* and the *dhyeya*.[18]

Goraksha-śataka (*GŚ*) devotes only five verses to *āsanas* selecting only *Siddhāsana* and *Kamlāsana* (*Padmāsana*) as the most important of the eighty-four *āsanas* and briefly describes them. Goraksha further says that one who is desirous of gaining perfection should know well the six *chakras*, the three lac *nāḍīs* and sixteen *ādhāras*, the nine doors (*nava dvāra* or the nine *randhras* of the sense organs), the five *vyomas*, the five tutelary divinities, the Meru (column) in his body.[19] The *Manḍala Brāhmaṇa Upanishad* also says, "He is a Yogin in name only who does not know well the *chakras*, the *ādhāras*, the three lac *nāḍīs* and the five *ākāśas*".[20] Gorakshanātha briefly discusses the position of the lotuses (*padma*) or *chakras*, the number of petals in each *chakra* — *chaturdala* or four leaved (lotus) in the *Ādhāra*, six leaved *Svādhishṭhāna*, in the navel ten-leaved, in the heart twelve-leaved, sixteen-leaved in the *Kanṭha* (throat) .... Two leaved between the eye-brows and one-thousand leaved lotus in *Brahmarandhra*, and also mentions the *yoni-sthāna* between the first *chakra* and *Svādhishṭhāna*. He also gives the position of the *mahāliṅgama* and *kanda-yoni* from which

---

[17] *Yoga Martanḍa*, vs.105.

[18] *Supra*, p. 70.

[19] *GŚ*, vss.13-14. These have been discussed at length in Ch.VIII.

[20] *Mandala Brāhmaṇa Upanishad*, IV, p.252 (*Thirty Minor Upanishads*, tr. Narayanasvami Aiyar).

originate seventy-two thousand *nāḍīs*, of which ten are chief *nāḍis* viz., *Īḍā* situated on the left side, *Piṅglā* on the right, *Sushumnā* between them, *Gāndhārī* in the left eye, *Hastijihvā* in the right eye, *Pushā* in the right ear, *Yaśasvinī* in the left ear, *Alambushā* in the mouth, *Kuhuśa* in the region of the lung and *Saṅkhinī* in the *Mūlādhāra*.[21] The knowledge of *nāḍīs, chakras* etc., is essential for understanding both the philosophy and the practices of *Haṭha-Yoga*, and also for *tattva-bodha*. As Gopinath Kavirāj says, knowledge of *Para-pinḍa* as well as that of *sva-pinḍa* is necessary for *kāya-siddhi* which leads to *Paramapada* and the state of *nirutthāna*.[22]

We have noted earlier that the knowledge of *chakras, ādhāras, lakshyas* and *vyoma* is helpful, and even essential for one purpose or the other, but most of all in the rise of the *Kuṇḍalinī Śakti* to *Sahasrāra* when the *Sādhaka* identifies with these *chakras*, the seats of different forces of the *Mātṛikā-Śakti*, so that the influence of these forces binding him ceases and he passes from one centre of force to another until he identifies himself with Paramātmā and is liberated. Their knowledge is also useful in the concentration of mind, so important in *dhāraṇā, dhyāna* and *samādhi*.[23]

It will be useful to give some additional information about the *chakras* and *nāḍīs* as they figure conspicuously in the account of the awakening of the *Kuṇḍalinī Śakti* which rises up through the *Chitriṇī nāḍī* and "*disappears in the infinity of the Absolute*" in the *Sahasrāra* situated at the crown of the head, but, before doing so, it will be better to take up in the briefest possible manner an important concept of this sect viz., the presence of *Brahmāṇḍa* or the cosmos in the *pinḍa* (body).

---

[21] *Gorakha-Śataka*, vss.15-31.

[22] *Bhārtīya Sādhanā kī Dhārā*, p.104; *Śri-tattva chintāmaṇi*, p.319 in *The Six Centres and the Serpent Power* (*SCSP*).

[23] Supra, p.47.

It is described in the second *paṭala* of *Śiva-Saṃhitā* and has been discussed in detail in Gorakshanātha's *Siddha-siddhānta-paddhati* in his discourse on *Pinḍa-saṃvitti* i.e. understanding the *Pinḍa*. He says that the Yogī experiences the whole cosmic system consisting of animate and inanimate existences, the three *lokas* (viz. *Bhūr, Bhuvar, Svar*), the four higher worlds, different *lokas* (*Vishṇu loka, Śiva loka, Kula loka*, etc.), all the *devatās*, the seven oceans (*Kshāra, Kshīra, Dadhi* etc.), seven divisions of the world, the nine regions or *nava khanḍa*, all the eight mountains, the nine big rivers, trees or plants, all are conceived as dwelling in individual body, and gives their locations. *Viśvarūpa* exists in every individual, and an enlightened Yogī can see this *Viśvarūpa* not only in his own body, but in the body of every individual (macrocosm in microcosm) and therefore he is free from all fear or hatred or selfishness. In *Kālachakrayāna*, body is referred as epitome of the universe. *Śrī Kālachakratantrarāja* attempts to explain the whole *sṛishṭi* in the body and locates seas, rivers etc., in it.[24]

As discussed in detail in Chapter III, the idea of macrocosm being realisable in the microcosm helps a *yogī* in narrowing the field of his concentration to himself so that during *sādhanā* he may find that he is a complete solar system in himself, "and when he has known himself, he has known the universe which is but a self-unfoldment of His Śakti and the whole Cosmic order which he perceives in his own body is but manifestation of Śiva-Śakti and his self consciousness is completely absorbed in the Universal Consciousness."

Coming back to the *chakras*, which are, in the words of M.M. Gopinātha Kavirāj "intra-organic centres of spiritual energy",[25] and Feuerstein calls these as *psycho-energetic*

---

[24] Supra, pp.32ff; *Śiva-Saṃhitā*, II, vss.1-6; *SSP*, III, 1-12; *Kālachakratantrarāja*, Intro.

[25] Gopinath Kaviraj's paper *Chakras according to Gorakshanātha*, Saraswati Bhawan Series, Vol.II, 1923.

centers,[26] for some essential and relevant information before we proceed further. In most of the works we find mention of the six *chakras*, which are of major importance, viz., *Mulādhāra, Svādhisṭhāna, Maṇīpūra* (at the root of the navel), *Anāhata chakra* (in the heart and it is called *anāhata* because it is here that the sound of *Śabda Brahman* is heard), *Viśuddha* (at the base of the throat) and *Ājñā chakra* (between the eyebrows). In *Brahmarandhra*, in *Sahasrāra*, which is not a *chakra*, Supreme Consciousness (Śiva) dwells. But the number of these *chakras* is believed to be more than six, as described by M.M. Gopināth Kavirāj in his paper. Dr. Gopināth Kavirāj's findings were based on a manuscript of *Vairāṭa Purāṇa* and an old coloured chart obtained by him from a local person at Vārāṇasī interested in this *pantha*. Thus between *Svādhisṭhāna Chakra* and *Maṇīpūra* (in the navel), there are three distinct centers (*Sushumnā chakra* etc.) and there are six *chakras* beyond *Sahasrāra*.[27] In *Siddha-siddhānta-paddhati*, Goraksha mentions nine *chakras* (*Upadeśa* II).[28] Avalon (i.e. Sir John Woodroffe) cites a work written by Brahmānanda Swāmī, *Advaita Mārtanḍa*, in which there is mention of several *chakras* situated along the cerebro-spinal axis. Each of the major *chakra* has its own importance and meditation or *dhyāna* on these results in various benefits which are discussed in *Siddha-siddhānta-paddhati* and other works.[29]

As a part of the exercise to inform about the body, *Goraksha-Śaṭaka* states that the resting place of *prāṇa* is *Svādhisṭhāna Chakra*, and, of the seventy-two thousand *nāḍīs,* which originate from the *Kanda Yoni*, ten are the carriers of *prāṇa*. These are *Iḍā, Pingalā, Sushumnā, Gāndhārī* etc. *Goraksha-śataka* also states that *Iḍā*, *Pingalā*

---

[26] Feuerstein, *The Yoga Tradition*, p.534.

[27] Chakras according to Gorakshanātha, *loc.cit.*

[28] *SSP*, II, 1.

[29] *SSP*, II, 1-9.

and *Sushumnā* are conductors of *prāṇa* and that the presiding deity of *Iḍā* is moon, of *Pingalā* is sun and of *Sushumnā* fire, that *Iḍā* is situated on the left side, *Pingalā* on the right and *Sushumnā* in the middle. The *Goraksha-śataka* also describes the *vāyus* and their location and says that *Prāṇa* is the air of breathing which lies in the heart, *Apāna* is the downward going *vāyu* and *Samāna* the digestive air in the region of the navel, while *Vyāna* pervades the whole body, *Nāga* is the air (that functions in) eructation, *Kūrma* in winking, *Kṛkara* causes sneezing, *Devadatta* in yawning, *Dhanañjaya* pervades the whole body and does not leave even the dead body. These vital airs wade though all the *nādīs,* it says.[30] Gorakshanātha has given sufficient space and importance to the description of the *nāḍis*, the vital airs, etc.

Here we may take up three points only: (i) The position of *Iḍā, Pingalā* and *Sushumnā*, (ii) how *Sushumnā* serves as the carrier of *prāṇa* and (iii) how *prāṇa* has been conceived in the Nātha works. To put briefly, *Sushumnā*, which is inside the *Meru* (spinal column), extends from *Mūla* to the place of *Brahman* in the *Sahasrāra*. It is stated that inside *Sushumnā* is *Vajra nāḍī* and inside *Vajra nādī* is *Chitriṇī nāḍī* and within *Chitriṇī* is *Bahma nāḍī*, which is not really a *nāḍī* but the channel of *Chitriṇī* through which *Kuṇḍalinī Śakti* goes up to *Sahasrāra*. In the space *outside* the *Meru* are *Iḍā* on the left side and on the right *Pingalā. Iḍā* and *Pingalā* have also been described as *Yamunā* and *Saraswatī* and *Sushumnā* as *Gangā*. They meet at the space between the eyebrows, i.e. at the *Ajñā Chakra* and hence it is called *Triveṇī Yoga*, and bathing there is considered to be very meritorious. By bathing there is meant that when the "mind is suffused in the full knowledge of this *Ajñā Chakra*", it results in great merit.[31] There are many references to *Trikūṭa* or *Triveṇī* and *Sangama* in the *Nātha* literature and also that of the medieval Saints.

---

30 *Goraksha Śataka*, vss.33-41.

31 *Śri-tattva-chintāmaṇi* (*Shaṭ-chakra-nirūpaṇa*), p.322 in *SCSP*.

In the Buddhist Tantras, the nerve on the right (*Piṅgalā*) is identified as *Upāya* and the one on the left (*Iḍā*) as *Prajñā* and the middle one, the *Avadhūtī-mārga* or *Avadhūtikā*, is described as the path of *Sahaja*. "The two nerves on the left and right, may be said to represent the principle of duality and the *Sushumnā* or *Avadhūtikā* as the principle of absolute unity", says Shashibhushan Das Gupta in *Obscure Religious Cults*.[32]

As regards *prāṇa*, it may be admitted that it is not easy to define it in terms of modern sciences. The term is used for life, vitality, air or breath and it has been suggested that terms like *prāṇa-vāyu*, *sūkshma prāṇa-vāyu* suggest something more tangible than breath of expiration. *Prāṇa* has also been identified with *Spandana Śakti*, the subtle vibratory power penetrating the whole cosmos and is the cause of its creation. In the *Haṭha* texts, *prāṇa* is represented as a vital force "which surges through human body at a level more subtle than the bodily fluids".[33]

Earlier, we have noted that *prāṇa* is not breath as commonly suggested; it is the "sum total of cosmic energy in each body and its outward manifestation is the motion of lungs which is caused by *prāṇa* drawing in the breath or when expelling it".[34] M.M. Gopināth Kavirāj describes *prāṇa* as the first result of motion (*chalana*) and vibration (*spandana*) and it occurs before the emergence of *buddhi*. Its natural *dharma* or nature is *ucchāraṇa*.[35]

It is held that *Kuṇḍalinī* and *prāṇa*, both denote 'primal force' or energy though *Śakti Kuṇḍalinī* has also been described as an impulse that produces 'motion' and *vāyu* (*prāṇa*) as the medium of action, and that *Kuṇḍalinī* provides the static background which supports and gives rise to that

---

[32] *Obscure Religious Cults*, pp.91-92.

[33] Mikel Burley, *Haṭha-Yoga*, p.177-78.

[34] *Supra*, p.64.

[35] Gopinath Kaviraj's *Tāntrika Sādhanā aur Siddhānta*, p.222.

energy (*prāṇa*). It has also been observed that '*prāṇa devatā*', one of the titles of *Kuṇḍalinī* not only suggests relation between the two but also *Kuṇḍalinī*'s priority over *prāṇa*.[36] In *Gorakshabodha*, Gorakshanātha asks his guru, Matsyendra, "From where does *prāṇa* (or vital force) rise?" and the latter replies, "From the *śunya* (the ever revolving one)". "Where does *prāṇa* dwell in the body (*piṇḍa*)?" asks Goraksha. Maatsyendra, "*Prāṇa* dwells in the body harmoniously all through and is ever *chaitanya*". Goraksha, "Who sleeps and who wakes (all the eight *prahars*)?" Matsyendra, "*Mana* seems to sleep in *suśupti* but *pavana* (*prāṇa-vāyu*) remains awake or *chetana* (all the eight *prahars*)." [37] These are some of the questions concerning *prāṇa* only but in *Gorakhabodha* the great *Yogī* asks several questions of great philosophical import in just two-three lines and the master's answers are even more brief but carrying profound meaning.

Goraksha-Śataka also speaks about Ajapā *mantra* or Ajapā Gāyatrī which is discussed at some length by Goraksha. He says that the *Jīva* (in the form of *prāṇa*) goes out with the sound *ha* and enters the body again with the sound *sa*. The *Jīva* is always reciting this *mantra Haṃsa, Haṃsa* with every round of expiration and inspiration, i.e. Ajapā Gāyatrī. Mere desire to recite this *mantra* frees one from all sins. It says that Gāyatrī has sprung from *Kuṇḍalinī* and is *prāṇadhārinī* (supporter of *prāṇa*) and that the knowledge of *prāṇa* is *mahāvidyā*.[38]

Gorakshanātha's guru Matasyendra, says in *Kaula-Jñāna-Nirṇaya* that uttering the expression *haṃsa haṃsa* bestows *Moksha* and that the three worlds and the universe have emanated from Him. At another place in the same work

---

[36] Swami Ram, *Path of Fire and Light*, Vol.I: *Advanced Practices of Yoga* in Mikel Burley, *Haṭha-Yoga*, p.177.

[37] *Gorakhabodha*, 41-42, 63-64.

[38] *Goraksha-Śataka*, vss.42-46.

(*Patala* XVII) he says that *Haṃsa* lives within the body as *Kuṇḍalinī* which rises from the lowest zone until once more it is merged in *Dvādaśānta*. *Haṃsa* thus moves in the centre of the body, *nirlepa* (unattached), *nishkala* (pure), celestial, very subtle, immeasurable, inconceivable, ever blissful and though He is embryo of all, yet is free from birth. He is the Nātha, supreme, the essence of *Mahā-jñāna* or great knowledge, self-existent, both exhalation and inhalation, both *bhāva* and *abhāva*, ... Though *Haṃsa* moves in the living beings who are subject to happiness, unhappiness, bondage, death, hunger, delusion and other human failings, He himself is not affected by them. He cannot be cut or broken by any *chakra* nor he is subject to *rāga, mada, matsyara*, etc.[39]

To put in a simpler language, *Jīva* recites this *mantra* all the time during inhalation and exhalation. The sound sequence *Haṃsa-Haṃsa-Haṃsa* can also be heard as *So'ham-So'ham-Soham*, when reciting consciously, meaning "I am He". "Thus the body is constantly affirming its own true essence," as Feuerstein says.[40] And what is *Jīva*? In *Kulārṇavatantra* (IX, vs. 41), *Jīva* is described as "individuated consciousness deeming itself other than Omnipresent Divine, though in truth it is not a limited consciousness trapped in a material body but all comprising Being Consciousness".[41] In *Gorakhabodha*, Goraksha asks his Guru, "Where resides the *Jīva* in the body?" and Matryendra replies, "As *ghee* is immanent in milk, so *Jīva* is all pervasive in the body". At another place in the same work, Goraksha asks, "In which *Śūnya Jīva* is absorbed?" Matsyendra replies, "He is born in *Sahaja Śūnya*, Satguru gave him the knowledge of *Samīpa Śūnya* and he gets absorbed in *Atita Śūnya* i.e. *Mahā Śūnya*".. "And where does *Jīva* is absorbed after death?". Matsyendra replies,

---

[39] *Kaula-Jñāna-nirṇaya*, *Paṭala* VI, XVII.

[40] Feuerstein, *The Yoga Tradition*, p.421.

[41] *Kulārṇavatantra*, IX, vss.41-42.

"From *Sahaja* he comes, in *Sahaja* he is absorbed".[42] Matsyendra has described the state of *Sahaja* in *Akulavīra Tantram* (A.5, 11-14, 33-34 etc., Bagchi, Introduction, *Kaula-jñāna-nirṇaya*, pp.51-52).

According to the Tantras, "the individual (*Jīva*) becomes identical with the absolute (Śiva) after liberation and that there is no difference in essence between them. As N.K. Brahma points out (p.275) that the Tāntric view distinguishes it from that of the Bhakti schools "which agree in maintaining difference of some sort or other even after liberation". Also, the Tāntric view distinguishes itself from the Māyā-*vāda* of Śaṃkara, continues Brahma, by maintaining that "*Jīva bhāva* is real not illusory, and that many do actually come out of One".[43] Before liberation, however, as *Śiva-Saṃhitā* says, *Jīva* though possessed of many qualities is chained to the body by *karmas* including those amassed in the past life. In Kashmir Śaivism, *Jīva*, the individual Self is "*Chaitanya* or Śiva, the real Self of every individual, the very core of his being" whose physical aspects consists of *Pañchamahābhūtas* or *sthūla-śarīra* which is sustained by *prāṇa-Śakti* working in him. His psychic apparatus or *antaḥkaraṇa* consists of *manas* and *ahaṃkāra*. These three along with five *tanmātrās* form the *sūkshma śarīra* in which the soul leaves the body.[44]

In the Vernacular literature of the Nāthas, we frequently come across of the concept of *sūnya*. *Haṭha-Yoga-Pradīpikā* mentions (IV.70-73) four kinds of *śunya* as associated with the four stages or *avasthās* of *yoga* — *Ārambha*, *Ghaṭa*, *Parichaya* and *Nishpatti*. M.M. Gopinath Kaviraj has described *mahā-śūnya* as the feeling of *abhāva* (*abhāva-*

---

[42] *Gorakhabodha*, 29-30, 59-60. In *Akulavīra Tantram*, Matsyendranātha describes *Sahaja* as "Omniscient, omnipresent ... free from *bhāva* or *abhāva* (i.e. positive or negative attributes), self-existent, all pervading, beyond the reach of the illusory world". *KJN*, Intr. pp.51-52.

[43] N.K. Brahma, *Philosophy of Hindu Sādhana*, p.276.

[44] *Śiva Saṃhitā*, II, 38; *Śiva-Sūtras*, Intro. xxix.

bodha) of Śakti about to fulfil Her desire (*ichchā*) to create the *sṛishṭi*.[45]

Haṃsa Upanishad says, "In the *Ajapā mantra Haṃsa Soham, Haṃ* is the *bīja*, *Sa* is Śakti and *Soham* is the *kīlak* (wedge) to which the whole *mantra* is fastened". It further says that the *Ajapā mantra* leads to the state of *Unmanī*, and ultimately to hearing of *Nāda*.[46] The attainment of the *unmanī* state is the aim of all Tantras. In this state "all attachment prompted by *manas* towards worldly things is dispelled and *māyā* ceases completely".[47] Viśvanātha quoting *Svacchanda-Saṃgraha* says that in this stage (of *dhyāna*) there is no cognition of anything, no distinction is made between *kāla* and *kalā* and there is "no cessation of continuity" in the identity of Self with the Supreme Spirit. *Unmanī* represents the highest aspect of '*Parā-Śakti*'. *Haṭha-Yoga-Pradīpika* says (IV.103), "*tattva* is the seed, *Haṭha* the *kshetra* (field) and *Vairāgya* the water. By the action of these three, the creeper *unmanī* thrives very rapidly". It says that the absorption produced by *Nāda* at once leads to *unmanī* state.[48]

Haṃsa is described as "that manifestation of *Nāda* which is symbolic of life. The *Anāhata Nāda* in its inner significance is symbolic of *Praṇava* (*Oṁ*)". By the intense awareness of this *Prāṇava* there arise nine stages of Yoga which are subtle forms of *Nāda*. The ninth stage is *unmanī* which is the highest stage of consciousness.[49] Up to the eighth stage (*samanā*) there can only be realisation of the true nature of Self (*ātma-vyāpti*). It is at the stage of *unmanī* that there can be *Śiva-vyāpti* or "the realisation of the world as an aspect of Self". Another name of *unmanī* is *Sahaja-vidyā*.[50]

---

45 *Haṭha-Yoga-Pradīpikā*, IV, 70-73.

46 *Haṃsa Upanishad*, (*Thirty Minor Upanishads*, tr. K.N. Aiyar), p.213.

47 *Śiva-Sūtras*, Intro. lv.

48 *Haṭha-Yoga-Pradīpikā*, IV, 79, 103.

49 *Śiva-Sūtras*, Intro. lv.

50 *Ibid.*

Goraksha in *Goraksha-śataka* devotes eleven verses to *Kuṇḍalinī*, from which, he says, Gāyatrī is sprung. He describes how coiled around the *Kanda* She lies asleep with Her face covering the Brahmadvāra, and how on being awakened through union of *manasa* and *māruta* (*prāṇa-vāyu*), She rises through the *Sushumnā*. Just as a door is forced open (*haṭhāta*) by a key without any effort, it says, in the same way a *Yogī* breaks open the *moksha-dvāra* or the door of release by means of *Kuṇḍalinī*.[51] A similar description is found in all the *Haṭha* texts. *Goraksha-Śataka* states that *Kuṇḍalinī* is set in motion by certain *mudrās* such as *Mahāmudrā*, *Uḍḍiyāna-bandha, Khecharī mudrā* etc. He briefly describes (vss. 57-82) these *mudrās* and their benefits and states that the *Yogin* who knows the *Śaktichālana mudrās* is ready for *mukti* (release).[52]

Haṭha-Yoga-Pradīpikā (III.53-111) has discussed these *muḍras*, and bandha in considerable detail. Emphasising the unique importance of *Khecharī mudrā*, it says that there is only one seed from which the whole *sṛishṭi* (universe) grew and there is only one *mudrā* called *Khecharī*, there is only one *deva* (God) without any support (*nirālamba*) and there is only one state (*avasthā*) i.e. *manonmanī*. About *Uḍḍiyāna bandha* it says (III.54) that it so called "because by its practice, the *prāṇa-vāyu* 'flies' (flows) in the *Sushumnā*, and ranks it as the best of all the *Bandhas*. About the *Mūla-bandha*, it says that by it, the sleeping *Kuṇḍalinī* on being woken up, becomes straight, and enters the *Brahmanāḍi* just as a serpent enters its hole".[53]

In *Amaraughaprabodha*, Goraksha highly praises *Mahāmudrā*; by practising it, he says, one can become a *siddha-purusha*.[54] *Śiva-Saṃhitā* says that by practising any

---

[51] *Gorakha-Śataka*, vss.47-57.

[52] *Ibid.*, vss.57-82.

[53] *Haṭha-Yoga-Pradīpikā*, III, vss.53-111.

[54] *Amaraugha Prabodha*, vss.29-33; *Śiva-Saṃhitā*, IV, 18.

one of the ten *śakti-chālana mudrās* according to the instructions of the *Guru* and *Yoga-śāstra*, one becomes a *Siddha*.[55]

The idea of *Kuṇḍalinī Śakti* is fundamental to *Haṭha Yoga*. As *Haṭha-Yoga-Pradīpikā* says, all the *Tantras* and *Yoga*-practices rest on *Kuṇḍalinī* just as Śeshanāga is the support of the earth with all the mountains etc.[56] In *Shaṭ-Chakra Nirūpaṇa*, Sri Pūrṇānanda Yati says that *Kuṇḍalinī* or Devi as *Śabda-Brahman* is the world of body (*Pinḍānda*) or *kshudra-Brahmāṇḍa* (microcosm) which maintains all the beings in the world by inhalation and exhalation. She is described as creation itself "in whom dwells creation, existence and dissolution".[57] *Kuṇḍalinī Śakti* or *Parāśakti* is "the central creative power of the entire *Mātṛikā* of all the subjective and objective phenomenon and expresses herself in three ways: *Paśyantī, Madhyamā* and *Vaikharī*". In all the Tantras She is described like lightening and is held to represent a reservoir of potential force or energy which is active in Her various levels of manifestation. In both the states, manifest as well as unmanifest, She is the Power of Śiva, infinite, dynamic, external during self-manifestation and immanent in the transcendent nature of Śiva, "a fathomless reservoir of latent energy into which the *Yogī* is considered to tap when he or she brings about elevation of *Kuṇḍalinī*".[58] As M.M. Gopīnāth Kavirāj observes, "The *Kuṇḍalinī-Śakti* when released from the obscuration of matter rises up spontaneously and disappears in the infinite of the Absolute. This disappearance does not mean annihilation, it simply means absorption and unification ..... Brahman is nothing but the eternity manifest. The difference between Śiva and Śakti is really a difference

---

[55] *Śiva-Saṃhitā*, IV, vss.57-58.

[56] *Haṭha-Yoga-Pradīpikā*, III, vs.1.

[57] *Śri-tattva-chintāmaṇi* (*Shaṭ-chakra-nirūpaṇa*), pp.318, n.3, 347-350 in *The Six Centres and the Serpent Power* (*SCSP*).

[58] *Śiva Sūtras*, p, 95; Mikel Burley, *Haṭha-Yoga*, p.178-79.

without any distinction".[59] In *Siddha-siddhānta-paddhati*, Gorakshanātha has described in various ways the eternal and essential union between Śiva and Śakti i.e. "between the Supreme Transcendent Spirit or Consciousness and Supreme all-originating Power. Śakti is infinite and eternal dynamic Power inherent in the transcendent nature of Śiva and She is self-manifestation of Śiva in the form of continuous evolution. In His transcendent nature Śakti is hidden (*avyakta*) in Him".[60] We have discussed in considerable detail the nature of *Kuṇḍalinī* and account of Her journey to the *Sahasrāra* earlier.[61]

After discussing briefly *Mahāmudrā, Khecharī Mudrā* and three *bandhas* viz., *Jālandhara, Mūlabandha* and *Uḍḍiyāna bandha* Goraksha devotes the last ten verses of *Gorakshaśataka* to *Praṇāyāma*.[62] These *bandhas* and *mudrās* restrain breath leading to steadiness of mind. Some of the principal *mudrās* are called *bandha* (*Mūla, Jālandhara Uḍḍiyāna* etc.). Among the *mudrās*, *Śaktichālana* and *Śāmbhavī* are important.

Gheranḍa Saṃhitā's third *Upadeśa* (vss.1-95) is devoted to the description of 25 *mudrās*, including *Mahāmudrā, Uḍḍiyāna bandha, Mahā-vedha, Khecharī mudrā, Yoni-mudrā. Śaktichālana mudrā* and *Śāmbhavī mudrā* and vss.94-100 are devoted to the benefits bestowed by the *mudrās*.[63] *Haṭha-Yoga-Pradīpikā* also devotes a major part of the third *Upadeśa* to the description of the *mudrās*.[64] The main aim of the *mudrās* is to assist in the awakening of *Kuṇḍalinī* and to make it move upwards in the *Sushumnā* towards the

---

[59] Gopinath Kaviraj's paper, Some Aspects of History and Doctrines of the Nāthas, *Saraswati Bhawan Series*, Vol.VI, 1927.

[60] A.K. Banerji, *Philosophy of Gorakhnātha* (*PGN*), p.63.

[61] See Ch.VI.

[62] *Goraksha-Śataka*, vss.90-100.

[63] *Gheranḍa Saṃhitā*, III, 1-100.

[64] *Haṭha-Yoga-Pradīpikā*, III, 1-94.

Sahasrāra. The awakening of *Kuṇḍalinī* and Her journey to *Sahasrāra* piercing the *chakras* and *granthis* is of the highest importance, in fact essential for attaining *Amaraugha Siddhi* and thereby ending all feeling of duality. It will be noted that *Prāṇāyāma, Mudrā* etc., all have only one aim i.e. to facilitate the attainment of *Rāja-yoga* by arousing and intensifying the spiritual power (*Kuṇḍalinī*) latent in every person so that it is united and finally absorbed in the Supreme Transcendent Spirit in which state one realises the non-difference between the *Ātmā* and the *Paramātmā*. *Haṭha-Yoga-Pradīpikā* says (IV.71) that a *yogī* "whose *Kuṇḍalinī* has awakened and who has renounced all *karmas* attains *Sahajāvasthā*".[65]

Goraksha says that so long as *vāta* (air) moves, *chitta* also moves. *Chitta* becomes stationary (*niśchala*) when *vāyu* ceases to move. Therefore, a *Yogin*, by restraining the (*vāyu*) should acquire immovability.[66] As Gopinātha Kavirāj writes, "The essence of *Haṭha-Yoga* lies in the conquest of *vāyu*. It is an article of universal acceptance in this country that *bindu* (*śukra* or seminal fluid), *vāyu* (intra-organic vital currents) and *manas* (mind or thinking principle) are closely related, and by restraining one of them the remaining two may be easily held in check. The restraint of *bindu* through the practice of *Brahmacharya* being assumed, the *Haṭha Yogins* direct the control of *vāyu* ..... as a means for the realisation of mental quiescence which is the ultimate aim of all striving".[67]

Gorakhsha-Śataka states that when the whole *nāḍī-chakra* (system of *nāḍīs*) full of secretions is purified by (*prāṇāyāma*), then the yogin becomes capable of restraining *prāṇa*. "By cleansing the *nāḍis*" he says in the last verse of his work "the *prāṇa* is restrained as described ..... and the *Nāda* is heard".[68]

---

[65] *Ibid.*, IV, 11.

[66] *Goraksha Śataka*, vs.90.

[67] Gopinath Kaviraj's paper, Some Aspects of History and Doctrines of the Nāthas.

[68] *Goraksha-Śataka*, VI, 95, 101.

The *Nāda* or *Śabda* is regarded as *Kuṇḍalinī Śakti* Herself "manifested as sound or vibration, one of Her titles being Śabda Brahman, and as She ascends so the sound becomes increasingly refined and Yogin's mind more fully absorbed in it. By fixing one's attention, dissolution of *chitta-vṛittis* or mental modifications is brought about resulting in *laya,* which is the main aim of *yoga*". *Haṭha-Yoga-Pradīpikā*[69] gives the various stages of *Nāda*, as it is heard.

Nāda has been described as the primal sound (*śabda*), which is heard as an inner sound when meditation reaches a certain stage. It is transcendental sound, which is *anāhata*. The *anāhata* (*anāhata nāda* of the Bhakti Saints) has been regarded as *Brahma rūpa* because it is *śāśvata* i.e. eternal. It arises during the course of deep meditation. In the Nātha literature there are several references to it. *Nāda-bindu-Upanishad* has described the various sounds, which get more and more subtle and are heard at different levels of meditation. It says, "The sound proceeding from *Praṇava*, which is Brahman, is of the nature of effulgence; the mind becomes absorbed in it. The sound exists till there is *ākāśic* conception (*ākāśa saṃkalpa*). Beyond this is the soundless (*aśabda*) Para Brahman which is Paramātman",[70] it says. In *Gorakhabodha* Matsyendra tells Goraksha, "When *Nāda* is heard in the innermost depths of mind, it elevates the adept to the highest spiritual plane and he attains the state of *samādhi*". Intense awareness of *Nāda* is called *Dhvani Yoga*, a very ancient form of *Yoga*.[71]

The *Nāda* sounds are believed to issue from the *Anāhata chakra* in the cardiac region "for it is here that the *Śabda Brahman*, manifested by *vāyu* and in association with *Buddhi*,

---

[69] *Haṭha-Yoga-Pradīpikā*, IV, 83-101.

[70] *Nāda-bindu-Upanishad* (in *Thirty Minor Upanishads*), p.257; Cf. *Haṭha-Yoga-Pradīpikā*, IV, 64-101.

[71] *Gorakhabodha*, 62. For a detailed discussion on *Nāda*, see *Tāntrika Sādhanā aur Siddhānta*, pp.218-38. Intense awareness of *Nāda* is called *Dhvani-yoga*, a very ancient form of *Yoga* (*Śiva-Sūtras*, liii).

and of the nature of manifested *Nāda*, endowed with a special motion (*vishesha-spanda*), exists in *Madhyamā* speech". It may be mentioned that though sound (*śabda*) is not audible by gross senses till it is in the form of *vaikharī* speech, the *yogī* is believed to hear "the subtle *Nāda* when with the help of various *bandhas* and *mudrās*, *Prāṇa* and *Apāna* are united in the *Sushumnā*.[72]

Why *Nāda* occupies such an important place in the Tantras and in the Nātha works in particular? It is because, as S.N. Dasgupta suggests, "The Tantras assume that the movement which has produced the world is represented in us in miniature in the production of sound. The process of production of sound is the epitome of the notion as it were of the cosmic process of creation. The same process which underlies the cosmic creation manifests itself in us in every case of the production of sounds, so that the genesis of sounds is not to be taken as imaginary but a real symbol of the creative process". He points out that "*Śabda* or sound has been regarded as eternal since the very beginning of the philosophic speculation in India, such as in the Mīmāṃsā School, but while there *śabda* is regarded as inanimate (*achetana*), in *Tantra* it is conceived as containing within itself *jñāna* (thought), *ichchā* (will) and *kriyā* (movement).[73]

The information contained in *Goraksha-Śataka* thus makes it an important text for understanding *Haṭha-Yoga* and also the Nātha philosophy. All subsequent works on *Haṭha-Yoga* seem to have elaborated the concepts and methods delineated in *Goraksha-Śataka*, though for details, they seem to have drawn information from other works on *Yoga* also, especially the *Yoga-sūtra* and *Siddha-siddhānta-paddhati*.

---

[72] A. Avalon, (John Woodroffe), *The Six Centres and the Serpent Power*, pp.220-221.

[73] S.N. Dasgupta, *Philosophical Essays*, pp.164-165.

Chapter X
CONCLUSION

The problem of the Eighty-four Siddhas, presence of the names of some of the Nātha Siddhas in the list of Vajrayānī-Sahajayānī Siddhas, as well as the puzzle of the several lists of the *Nava-Nāthas* which do not fully agree with each other has engaged the attention of several eminent scholars for the past many years. Thus the names of Matsyendranātha, Gorakshanātha, Jālandharanātha, Charpaṭi, Kānipā, etc., occur in the list of the Nātha Siddhas given in *Varṇa Ratnākara* as well as in the list of the Eighty-four Siddhas compiled by Rahul Sānkṛatyāyana from the Buddhist sources. This can be explained, to some extent, by the similarity in many concepts of the Śaiva Tantras and those of the Vajrayānī Buddhist, which tended on the one hand to blur the identity of the sect or philosophical system to which many Siddhas belonged, and, on the other hand, also tended to enhance their acceptability in systems other than to which they strictly speaking belonged. As regards the Nava-Nāthas, what is important is that they are reverently remembered even today, and their names are spoken when counting the beads, as *avatāras* or incarnations, and as the most sacred ones for the Nāthas. The Nāthas recite a prayer "*Nava Nātha Svarūpa Darśana*" on different occasions, and worship of the Nine Nāthas and Eighty-four Siddhas is performed at the end of the initiation ceremony of a novice.

It is a curious fact that though there is considerable information about the philosophy of Matsyendranātha and his great disciple Gorakshanātha, mainly through their works, there has been a prolonged controversy about their precise period and their original home. After examining the available information it seems that Matsyendra lived about 1050 A.D. or so and Gorakshanātha can be assigned to the first half of the 12th century. Matsyendra's *Kaula-jñāna-nirṇaya* gives the most detailed account of his philosophy though *Akulavīratantrama* and *Jñānakārikā* are also helpful.

The Nātha *sampradāya* is against all rituals and externalities. This is clear from the works of both Matsyendra and Gorakshanātha. When discussing the nature of *Akulavīra*, Matsyendranātha enjoins the worship of the *mānas Liṅga* which is *aprameya* and eternal, the cause of creation (*sṛishṭi*) and its dissolution, by offering mental flowers, the first flower being *Ahiṃsā*, the second control over the senses, the third compassion, fourth right disposition, the fifth flower offering is forgiveness, the sixth suppression of anger, the seventh *dhyāna* (meditation) and the eighth *jñāna* (knowledge of the true Self). In *Kaulajñānanirṇaya* (*Paṭala*, xxiv), he makes a distinction between external and internal worship. In *Siddha-Siddhānta-Paddhati*, we find Gorakshanātha laying great emphasis on the need to eradicate the *vikāras* from the body, the sense organs and mind, and on realisation of the Universal Consciousness through *ātma-jñāna* rather than taking recourse to ritualistic formalities and externalities.

The first *upadeśa* in *Siddha-Siddhānta-Paddhati* amply shows that the Nātha Mahā Yogīs had tried to understand the process of creation (*sṛishṭi*) very minutely. This has been discussed at length in Ch.I of the present work. The main concept is that by the mere will of Para Brahman or Parama Śiva to create, the Parā-Śakti, which inheres in Him causes Divine pulsation in Para Brahman and activates *Aparā-Śakti* which assists in the creation of *sṛishṭi*. Then follows a very detailed classification of the attributes of Nijā-Śakti, Parā-Śakti, Kuṇdalinī-*Śakti* and of the attributes of the five *tattvas* of *Anādi-pinḍa* viz., *Aparampara* (Sadā-Śiva), *Paramapada* (Paramātma), *Śūnya, Nirañjana*, and of the stages of the evolution of *Ādya-Piṇda Purusha* from the Cosmic body etc. We note that while the Vedāntists regard the world of *Mahābhūtas*, from which *sṛishṭi* was created, as having only illusory existence born of *Māyā* or Avidyā "and the Supreme Spirit, Brahman, as *adhishṭhāna* of this illusion", Gorakshanātha and the Mahāyogīs regard the world observable to us as a "self-manifestation and embodiment of the Supreme Spirit, by virtue of the real power (*Śakti*) inherent in Him".

Here is a very serious attempt to understand the role of the Ultimate Reality in the process of creation of *sṛishṭi*, and of the human beings, the working of human mind and the factors, which influence the behaviour and conduct of an individual etc. Whether it is the discussion of the nature of *Paramapada* or *Sāmarasya* or *Sahaja-Jñāna*, or the need of a *Sadguru*, an analytical approach, marked by reason and objectivity, is observed. There is mention of *Siddhis* or occult powers but it is advised not to attach importance to these but to strive for realising the *Paramapada*. The *pantha,* in which caste has no place, advocates a vigorous active life, a conduct beyond reproach and to be conscious of non-difference between the individual body and the Cosmic body, thus giving hope even to the weakest and the lowliest, who can, by intensive awareness and mental observation of one's own true nature, by deep meditation and reflection and by following the *Yoga-mārga* can realise *Paramapada*, indescribable even by scholars who have acquired mastery in the exposition of most subtle ideas. The *Yama, Niyama, Āsana, Prāṇāyāma, Pratyāhāra, Dhāraṇā* and *Dhyāna* only serve to assist in intensive awareness and observation of one's own true nature which is non-different from the Supreme Soul realisable in the state of *Samādhi.*

Another fundamental concept of the Natha philosophy is that macrocosm is realisable in the microcosm. As Goraksha says, 'The *Yogī* who experiences the whole Cosmic system, including all the animate and inanimate existences, within the individual body, is the perfect knower of the body. According to Goraksha, *Viśvarūpa* Parameśvara Paramātmā resides in every individual body and a *Yogī* can behold or perceive that *Viśvarūpa* not only in his own body but in the body of every other individual. This makes him, he says, free from all fear, envy or hatred towards others.

Gorakshanātha discusses *Ashṭāṅga Yoga* rather briefly. In describing *Yama, Niyama, Āsana* and even *Prāṇāyāma* and *Pratyāhāra*, he gives only the central idea behind these *aṅgas*. At places he is even more brief than Patañjali whose *Yoga-Sūtra* is required to be consulted frequently to fully understand the significance of Goraksha's observations. As we proceed further with his main work on the philosophy viz., *Siddha-Siddhānta-Paddhati*, it becomes clear that the *Yoga-mārga* of Goraksha is deeply steeped in the ancient *yogic* traditions of India traceable, in varying degrees, to the *Vedas, Upanishads, Smṛitis, Yoga-Sūtra, Purāṇas* and other works. Gorakshanātha never even alludes that he is deviating from the spiritual and philosophical traditions of the country, not to say of revolting against them. He held that it was necessary to synthesise the views of different schools of philosophy so as to achieve the state of *viśrānti* which marks the cessation of all *chitta-vṛittis* and then the *yogī* is absorbed in Para-Brahman Parameśvara.

Gorakshanātha gives highest importance to *sāmarasya* or identity with Paramapada Paramātmā. The terms *Paramapada, śūnya* etc., occur frequently in the Nātha literature and that of the medieval Bhakti saints. What is *Paramapada* and how can it be realised? He says that *Paramapada*, which is *svasaṁvedya*, indescribable, unknowable through intellect, is realisable only by intensive awareness and mental observation of one's true nature which leads to the recognition of the non-difference between the individual body and the Supreme Cosmic body, wherein the attributes of each of the five Divine Śaktis – *Nijā, Parā, Aparā, Sūkshmā* and *Kuṇḍalinī* are present. This experience of complete non-difference between the individual body (sva-*piṇḍa*) and Supreme Cosmic body (*Para-piṇḍa*) leads to the state of *Nirvyuthāna* or *Sāmarasya*. This experience leads to *ātma-jñāna* and knowledge of non-difference between the *Jivātmā* and the Paramātmā, thereby ending the feeling of duality between the individual body and the cosmic body, and *Paramapada*, the *akhaṇḍa*, self-luminous Universal Consciousness manifests in all its transcendental glory. Gorakshanātha lays great emphasis on the ideal of *Samarasakaraṇa* or absorption in the Supreme Consciousness and seems to assign it a stage higher than *Samādhi*. On realising *Paramapada*, Goraksha says, the whole universe is perceived as *Paramātma-svarūpa*.

Gorakshanātha considers *Yoga-mārga* as superior to all other paths since, according to him, it is the bestower of *moksha* and leads to *Paramātma bodha* or the realisation of the Supreme Spirit. The same object of *Yoga* is implied in the *Yoga-sūtra* (I, 2-4). Thus *Sutra* I.3 says that when through *Yoga, chitta-vṛittis* are controlled, the *seer* (*Purusha*) can see his own true nature which at other times the *seer* identifies with the *vṛittis*. In *Gorakshapaddhati*, *Yoga-Śāstra* is described as the fruit of the *Vedas* which are like *Kalpavṛiksha*. Eminent scholars such as M.M. P.V. Kane have shown that the origin of the *Yoga* system can be traced to the *Vedas* and much more clearly in the *Upanishads, Mahābhārata, Bhagvad-Gītā, Smṛitis* and *Purāṇas*. Goraksha's observation counters the tendency noticed in some works which indirectly try to underrate study of the *Vedas*. This tendency was on account of strong opposition to the *Varṇa* system which had the approval of the *Śṛutis*.

Goraksha attaches highest importance to *Rāja-Yoga* without which, he says in *Amaraughaprabodha*, one cannot achieve *deha-siddhi* nor *Īśvara-siddhi*. *Gheranḍa Saṃhitā* and some other works clearly say that *Haṭha-Yoga* is "the first rung of the ladder that leads to *Rāja-Yoga. Haṭha-Yoga-Pradīpikā* says (IV.102) that "all the *upāya* (methods) of *Haṭha-Yoga* are meant for gaining success in *Rāja-Yoga*". At another place, it says that "no success is possible in *Rāja-Yoga* without *Haṭha-Yoga* and no success is possible in *Haṭha-Yoga* without *Rāja-Yoga* and so one should practise both till complete success is gained". *Śiva-Saṃhitā* also says the same and adds that the *yogī* should first learn *Haṭha-Yoga* under the instructions of a wise *guru*. It is, therefore, not surprising that Gorakshanātha chooses to delineate the fundamentals and methods of *Haṭha-Yoga* in *Gorakshaśataka*. Goraksha mentions four kinds of *yoga* — *Laya, Haṭha, Mantra* and *Rāja-Yoga* and the four stages of *yoga* which are common in all the four kinds, but for details about these stages we have to turn to *Śiva-Saṃhitā* and *Haṭha-Yoga-Pradīpikā*, for Gorakshanātha, like Patañjali, leaves the details to be taught by the *guru* of an aspirant. The same is the case with his account of the *Rāja-Yoga*. Though *Haṭha-Yoga-Pradīpikā* says that it is describing the practice of *Anāhatanāda* as propounded by Gorakshanātha for the benefit of those who are unable to understand the *Śāstras* and that it was the chief among the various methods for going into absorption, Goraksha himself does not go into details of the *Rāja-Yoga*. In the fourth stage of *Yoga* i.e. *Nishpatti* state, which comes when the Rudra *granthi* is pierced and the *anil* enters the seat of the Lord (*Śiva-pīṭha*), pleasant sound like that of a flute is heard. The absorption of *chitta* in this sound is the fulfilment of *Rāja-Yoga* which results in perpetual feeling of delight. The absorption (*laya*) produced by *nāda* gives rise to the *unmanī* state. By practice, the mind becomes steady in the *nāda* and is absorbed in it. When the sounds disappear, one realises Para-Brahman Paramātmā.

In consonance with the tradition of *Guru-vāda* in the Indian philosophy, in the Nātha *sampradāya* also, highest importance is attached to the need of a *sadguru*, a *guru* who is self-realised, who has deep insight into the five states of consciousness (*sthūla, sūkshma, kāraṇa, turīya* and *turyātīta*), and it is only by his grace that a *sādhaka* can realise *Paramapada*, says Goraksha. By his preachings, or even by his compassionate glance, a *guru* can destroy all the eight bonds of the aspirant i.e. *jarā, janma, mṛityu, vyādhi, kāma, krodha, mada, avidyā* and *ahaṃkāra*. Not only this, a *sadguru*, in a moment, by *Śaktipāta*, or even by his mere compassionate glance, can establish his disciple in *Ātma-svarūpa Paramapada*, says Goraksha.

What ideal an aspirant or *sādhaka* should have before him? This is best indicated in Gorakshanātha's description of an *Avadhūta*. He should have removed, says Goraksha, all the natural *vikāras* arising from the body, the sense organs and mind, whose every word is *Veda* i.e. full of knowledge, who has destroyed the web of the five afflictions — *avidyā* or primal ignorance, *asmitā* (egoism), *rāga* (intense desire), *dvesha* (envy) and *abhinivesha* (too much adherence), who has freed himself of manifold diversities of waking, dream and deep sleep states, who is entirely without fear, who shows others the path of welfare. An *Avadhūta* has the knowledge of the Supreme Spirit, continues Goraksha, and all his distinctive marks — *kuṇḍala*, ashes, *śelī, kharpara* etc., are symbolic of high spiritual and moral attainments. He is fully absorbed in the feeling of *nirvyuthāna* in which state he experiences oneness of individual soul and the Supreme Soul and he has realised within himself synthesis of all the different schools of philosophies, sects and religions. He is above the *āshrama*-system, and he symbolises in himself the true characteristics which the followers of various sects and orders — *Vaishṇava, Śākta, Vīra-Śaiva, Kāpālika, Sanyāsī, Yogī, Digambara*, etc., should really have and not merely external appearances. He illuminates the world by the light of his knowledge, is seeker of the Reality (*tattva-chintaka*) and seeks to understand and synthesise *Chāravāka, Arhat* (Jainism),

Bauddha, Nyāya, Vaiśeshika, Sāṃkhya, Mīmāṃsā and various other schools of philosophy. These are without doubt highest ideals and norms which Goraksha sets before one joining the Nātha sect, *Avadhūta* being the stage one should aspire to reach in his life.

The impression which prevails in some quarters of *Haṭha Yoga* being more concerned with the body, or that it incorporates only the lower or physical elements and is not a spiritual discipline, is amply disproved by nearly all the Nātha works including those which are mainly on *Haṭha-Yoga*, such as *Gorakshaśataka, Haṭha-Yoga Pradīpikā, Gheraṇḍa Saṃhitā*, etc. In fact, the philosophy of the sect and supreme aim of all efforts find ample expression in these works also. As *Haṭha-Yoga-Pradīpikā* says that all the *upāya* (methods) of *Haṭha-Yoga* are meant for gaining success in *Rāja-Yoga* which leads to the realisation of the Para-Brahman Paramātmā by absorption of *chitta* in the *nāda*. Gorakshanātha emphasises that an aspirant should know his body well, the knowledge being essential for *Kāya-sādhana*. "He is a *Yogī* in name only", he says, "who does not cognize well the *chakras, ādhāras*, the three lac *nāḍīs*, ..." The *chakras* influence the direction of the flow of energy and represent different planes of spiritual experience. They are not physical constituents. In *Yoga*, especially in *Haṭha Yoga* the concept of *chakra* or the symbolic idea of *chakra* plays a vital role. The number of these *chakras* has been given differently by different authors. Of these, six are vital centres within the spinal column. The *chakras* are the seats of different forces of the *Mātṛikā-Śakti*. In fact, there are two points of view in understanding the *chakras, nāḍīs* the ascent of the *Kuṇḍalinī Śakti* in the *Sushumnā* on way to the *Sahasrāra*, the nature of *prāṇa* etc. — (1) that of the Siddhas and traditional Yogic approach and (2) attempts by some of the scholars, such as M.M. Gopinatha Kaviraj, Sir John Woodroffe, Hinze and a few others who have tried to understand the *chakras, Kuṇḍalinī* etc., in the light of modern scientific knowledge. Both these approaches have been taken into account in the preceding chapters.

The search for truth and Reality, emphasis on the need to confirm according to the real meaning of the various terms rather than to their outward symbols and appearances, an approach marked by understanding of other sects and schools of thought are distinguishing features of the Nātha philosophy and should serve as an example to other religions, sects and religious orders, specially those which claim exclusive knowledge of the truth and Reality, and finality about their dogmas and beliefs. Nātha philosophy has thus great relevance for all cultures and countries.

We do not have enough sources for assessing correctly the role played by the Nātha *Sampradāya* during the 11th and the 12th centuries, during which this great sect appears to have emerged as an important factor on the Indian spiritual horizon. But, as noted elsewhere, it seems to have served as an effective counterpoise to *Vajrayāna*, which was attracting an ever increasing number of followers to its fold who were being lured by its intemperate approach and easy way of attaining *Mahā-sukha* through sex, and a little later, it seems to have served as a strong counter-poise to Islam also since caste had no place in the Nātha *sampradāya* and its monistic-dualistic concept of Brahman and emphasis on self-realisation of the Supreme Spirit without any external aid or agency, and on non-difference between the individual Self and Supreme Spirit, emphasis on mental worship and *dhyāna*, rejection of all superfluous externalities left no scope for Islam to claim superiority in the matter of societal values, there being no question of its claiming any superiority at the philosophical or spiritual level. The great impact of the Nātha philosophy on the medieval Bhakti Saints is very clear from their compositions, such as of Kabīr, because the Nātha philosophy as delineated by Goraksha in *Siddha-Siddhānta-Paddhati* and other works was flawless from spiritual and moral points of view, besides being in consonance with the *Upanishadic* traditions.

However, the Nātha *Sampradāya*, despite thousands of monasteries all over India throughout the medieval period and till our own times, could not capture as much popular imagination as the Gauḍīya or Vallabha *Sampradāya* could on account of their emotional appeal, colourful worship, and *Bhaktī-mārga* being easier to follow than the *Yoga-mārga*. Added to these was the neglect of the teachings and study of the Nātha texts round which the life and activities in the monasteries should have revolved and the Nātha *Yogīs* should have been moving about as learned monks confirming to the ideals set for an *Avadhūta* in the Sixth *Upadeśa* in the *Siddha-Siddhānta-Paddhati.* Even then, it has always been having far greater number of monasteries than any other *Sampradāya* in India, and its call to *yoga-mārga* for realising the non-difference between the individual soul and the Universal Soul has an eternal value for all human beings.

BIBLIOGRAPHY

Akulavīratantram, A. MS. Darbar Library, Nepal, ed. P.C. Bagchi in *Kaulajñānanirṇaya* (*KJN*), Calcutta, 1934.

Akulavīratantram B., MS. in the Collection of Gen. Keshar Samsher Jung Bahadur Rana, ed. P.C. Bagchi in *KJN*, Calcutta, 1934.

Amaraugha Prabodha, Gorakshanatha, in Kalyani Mallik's *Siddha-Siddhānta-Paddhati* (*SSP*) *and other Works of the Nātha Yogīs*, Poona, 1954.

Artistic Form and Yoga in the sacred Images of India, Heinrich Zimmer (tr. by G. Chapple and James B. Lawson, Oxford University Press, Delhi, 1984).

Bhārtīya Sādhanā kī Dhārā, Gopinath Kaviraj, Patna, 1984.

A Brief History of Tantra Literature, S.C. Banerji, Calcutta, 1988.

Charyāgīti Kosha, ed. Shanti Bhikshu Shastri, Calcutta, 1956.

Dharmaśastra kā Itihas, M.M. P.V. Kaṇe, (tr. Arjun Chaube Kasyapa), Vol.V, Lucknow, 1973.

Dhyānabindu Upanishad, tr. by K. Narayanasvami Aiyar in *Thirty Minor Upanishads*, Madras, 1914.

Dohā-Kosha, Rahul Sankratyayan, 2nd edn., Patna, 1997.

Essays and Lectures Chiefly on the Religion of the Hindus, A Sketch of the Religious Sects of the Hindus, H.H. Wilson, London, 1861.

Gheranḍa Saṃhitā, tr. Srisa Chandra Vasu, Oriental Reprint, 1975, First published in 1914-15.

Gorakha-bānī, ed. Pitambar Datta Badathval, Fifth Reprint, Ilahabad, 1994.

Gorakha-bodha, in *Natha Smpradaya aur Sukshma Veda* (*NSSV*), ed. Yogi Sawai Nath Sama, Paldi, 2004.

Gorakhnātha and the Kāṇphaṭā Yogīs, George Weston Briggs, Reprint, Delhi, 2001.

Goraksha Paddhati, tr. Mahidhar Sharma, Bambai, S.2011.

Gorakhnātha and Medieval Hindu Mysticism, Mohan Singh, Lahore, 1937.

Goraksha-Siddhānta-Saṃgraha (*GSS*) (with Commentary in Bhāshā), Dravyesh Jha Shastri, Pub. Mahant Purananathji, Bohar, 1938.

Goraksha-śataka, Poona Copy. Text in Briggs, *Gorakhnātha and Kānphaṭā Yogīs*, Reprint Delhi, 2001.

Goraksha-Siddhānta-Saṃgraha (*GSSP*), ed. Janardan Shastri Pandey, Varanasi, 1973. First published by M.M. Gopinath Kaviraj.

Gorakha Upanishad in Kalyani Mallik's *SSP and Other Works of the Nātha Yogīs*, Poona, 1954.

Goraksha Vachana Saṃgraha in A.K. Banerji's *Philosophy of Gorakhnatha*, Delhi, Reprint, 1988.

Haṭha Yoga Pradīpikā (*HYP*), tr. Pancham Sinh, *SSP* Edition, 1979.

Haṭha-Yoga — Its Context, Theory and Practice, Mikel Burley, Delhi, 2000.

History of Tāntric Religion, N.N. Bhattacharya, Delhi, 1987.

Jñānakārikā (MS) Darbar Library, ed. P.C. Bagchi, *KJN*, Calcutta, 1934.

Sri Kālachakratantra-rāja, ed. Biswanath Banerjee, Calcutta, 1993.

Kaulajñānanirṇaya and some Minor Texts of the School of Matsyendranātha (*KJN*), ed. P.C. Bagchi, Calcutta, 1934.

Kaulajñānanirṇaya, (tr.) Michael Magee, Varanasi, 1986.

The Krama Tāntricism of Kashmir, N. Rastogi, Delhi, Reprint 1996.

Nāda-bindu Upanishad, tr. K. Narayanasvami Aiyar, in *Thirty Minor Upanishads*, Madras, 1914.

Nātha Sampradāya, Hazari Prasad Dwivedi, Allahabad, 1996.

Nātha Sampradāya aur Sūkshma Veda (*NSSV*), compiled and edited by Yogi Sawai Nath Sama, Paldi, Sirohi, 2004.

Nātha Siddhon kī Bāniyān, ed. Hazari Prasad Dwivedi, Kashi, (1978).

Obscure Religious Cults, Shahibhushan Dasgupta, Calcutta, 1976.

An Outline of the Religious Literature of India, J.N. Farquhar, Delhi, Reprint 1967.

Paurānic and Tāntric Religion, J.N. Banerjee, Calcutta, 1966.

Philosophical Essays, Surendranath Dasgupta, Delhi,

Philosophy of Gorakhnātha, Akshaya Kumar Banerji, Reprint, Delhi, 1988.

Philosophy of Hindū Sādhanā, Nalini Kantha Brahma, London, 1932.

Rajasthān ke Nātha Sampradāya aur Sāhitya, ed. D.B. Kshirasagar and Nawal Krishna, R.O.R.I., Jodhpur, 1997.

Rāja Yoga, Swāmī Vivekānand, Kolkata, Reprint 2002.

Sabad, Kabir. *Kabir Vāṅgmaya*, Part II, ed. Jaideva Singh, Vasudeva Singh, Varanasi 2002.

Sādhanamālā, Vol.II, Benoytosh Bhattacharya, Baroda, 1968.

Sākhī, Kabir, *Kabir Vāṅgamaya*, Part III, ed. Jaideva Singh, Vasudeva Singh, Varanasi, 2000.

Śakti aur Śākta, Sir John Woodroffe, Reprint, Madras, 2001.

Śārīraka-Upanishad, in *Thirty Minor Upanishads*, Madras, 1914.

Saraswatī Bhawan Series, Vol.II, 1923, Vol.VI, 1927.

Siddha-Siddhānta-Paddhati (*SSP*), Gorakshanatha, in Kalyani Mallik's *SSP and other works of Nātha Yogīs*, Poona, 1954.

Siddha-Siddhānta-Paddhati Bhāratī, A Sanskrit Journal, (Special Number, November- December 2004, Jaipur)

Śiva Sūtras, Text and Commentary *Vimarśinī* of Kshemarāja tr. into English with exposition by Jaideva Singh, Delhi, Reprint 2003.

The Śiva Saṃhitā, tr. Srisa Chandra Vasu, SSP Edition, 1979.

The Six Centres and the Serpent Power, Arthur Avalon (Sir John Woodroffe)

Spanda-Kārikas (*The Kārikas and the Spanda-nirṇaya*), tr. into English by Jaideva Singh, Reprint, Delhi, 2001.

Śri-tattva-Chintāmaṇi, Purṇānanda Yati, *Shaṭ-chakra-nirūpaṇa* or the Description of the Six Centres, tr. Arthur Avalon.

Studies in Origin and Development of Yoga, Sures Chandra Banerji, Calcutta, 1995.

Studies in Tantras, Part I, P.C. Bagchi, Calcutta, 1939.

Sūkshma Veda in *Nātha Sampradāya aur Sūkshma Veda*, Paldi, Sirohi, 2004.

Tantra aur Āgama Shāstron kā Digdarshan, Gopinath Kaviraj (tr. Hans Kumar Tiwari), Patna, Reprint, 2003.

Tāntrika Bauddha Sādhanā aur Sāhitya, Nagendra Nath Upadhyaya, Kashi, 1958.

Tāntrika Sādhanā aur Siddhānta, Gopinath Kaviraj (tr. Hans Kumar Tiwari), Patna, 1994.

Tantras — Studies on their Religion and Literature, Chintaharan Chakravarti, Calcutta, 1963.

Tāntrika Vāṅgamaya men Śākta Dṛishṭi, Gopinath Kaviraj, tr. Hans Kumar Tiwari, Patna, 1994.

Tāntra Vidyā, Oskar Marcel Hinze (tr. from the original German by V.M. Bedekar), Delhi, Reprint 1997.

Thirty Minor Upanishads (*TMU*), tr. K. Narayanasvami Aiyar, Madras, 1914.

Vaishṇavism, Śaivism and other Minor Religious Systems, R.G. Bhandarkar, First Published in 1913, Reprint. Varanasi. 1965.

Vajranyānī Siddha Sarahapāda, Dvija Ram Yadava, Shantiniketan, 1980.

Yogamārtanḍa, in Kalyani Mallik's *SSP and Other Works of the Nātha Yogīs*, Poona, 1954.

Yoga-Sūtra, Patañjali, translation and commentary by Swami Vivekanand, in *Raja Yoga*, Kolkata, Reprint 2002.

Yoga-vishaya, in Kalyani Mallik's *SSP and Other Works of the Nātha Yogīs*, Poona, 1954.

The Yoga-Tradition — Its History, Literature, Philosophy and Practice, Georg Feuerstein, Prescott, Arizona, 1998.

Glossary of Technical Terms

A	:	
Abhiniveś	:	Too much adherence
Adaḥ	:	In the lower region
Advaita	:	Absense of duality; identity of Brahman or of Paramātman (Supreme Soul) with Jīvātmā or human soul
Ādya-piṇḍa-Purusha	:	First Cosmic personality of Śiva which emanates from Anādya-piṇḍa-Parameśvara and inheres the *svarūpa* of Paramānanda, Prabodha, Chidudaya, Chitprakaśa and Ahaṃbhāva.
Aṅga	:	Limb, part
Ahaṃkāra	:	I-making principle, I-feeling
Ahiṃsā	:	Non-violence (in thought, word and deed)
Ajapā – Gāyatrī mantra	:	Haṃsa, haṃsa automatically recited by Jīva with every round of expiration and inspiration which sounds as Soham, Soham i.e. "I am He".
Akhaṇḍa	:	Undivided
Akhaṇḍa antarjyoti	:	Light of the Self
Akula	:	Advaita form, beyond phenomenal differences; in Akula form Parā Śakti is non-different from Akula Śiva
Anādi	:	Having neither beginning nor end
Anādya-piṇḍa	:	Uncreated, all creating Divine Personality with Five constituent *tattvas (Aparampara, Paramapada, Śūnya, Nirañjana, Paramātmā)*
Antahkaraṇa	:	Inner psychic apparatus, the seat of thought and feeling

Antaraṅga : Interior aṅga of Yoga (Dhāraṇā, Dhyāna and Samādhi)

Anutthāna : State in which there is complete dissolution of mind and nothing arises in it

Aparā (Śakti) : The third stage of the self-unfoldment of Nijā-Śakti with some throbbing for self-expression or self-manifestation

Āsana : Posture — firm and pleasant; to establish oneself in I-Consciousness

Ashṭāṅga : Consisting of eight parts

Ātma-bodha : Knowledge of Soul (as non-different from the Supreme Spirit)

Ātma-jñāna : Knowledge of Self or Soul (being non-different from the Supreme Soul

Ātman : Individual soul, the Self

Ātma-svarūpa : Divine Self, true nature of Self

Ātma-tattva : The true nature of Soul

Atyāśramī : Not bound by the four stages of *Āśrama-dharma*, viz., Brahmacharya, Gṛihastha, Vānaprastha and Sanyāsa

Avidyā : Primal ignorance

B

Bahiraṅga : External, relating to the exterior; Five external *aṅga* of Yoga viz. Yama, Niyama, Āsana Prāṇāyāma and Pratyāhāra

Bandha : Yoga practice in which some parts of the body are contracted and 'locked'.

Bhāva : Existence, internal and external

Bhedā-bheda : Difference and the identity of God and the Universe

Bhūta-piṇḍa : Gross material body

Bhūtas : Original elements, gross physical elements

Brahman : Supreme Consciousness endowed with svātantrya Śakti i.e. unlimited power to know and do everything; Parama Śiva

Brahmāṇḍa : Cosmos, the universe

Brahma-mārga	:	The Path of realization of Brahman, i.e. Brahma nāḍī (inside Sushumnā) through which Kuṇḍalinī Śakti goes up to the Sahasrāra
Buddhi	:	Ascertaining intelligence; the power of forming and retaining conceptions and general notions
C		
Chaitanya	:	The Universal Soul; the foundational Consciousness which has absolute freedom of knowing and doing
Chakras	:	Intra-organic centres of spiritual energy; seats of vital energy which absorb and distribute *prāṇa*; represent different planes of spiritual experience, each symbolically represented by a lotus with fixed number of petals
Chidānanda	:	The nature of the Supreme Reality or Spirit consisting of consciousness and bliss
Chidrūpiṇī	:	Pure Consciousness
Chit	:	The Absolute; foundational Consciousness
Chit-prakāśa	:	The light of Supreme Consciousness
Chit-svarūpa	:	Universal Consciousness
Chitta	:	Empirical mind
Chitta-vṛittis	:	Mental modifications
Chitta-viśrānti	:	Cessation of thought-constructs (chitta-vṛittis)
D		
Dhāraṇā	:	Sixth aṅga of Yoga; holding the mind on to a particular place, object or point either in the body or outside
Dhyāna	:	Meditation during which there is no consciousness of effort to concentrate but duality exists between the person who is meditating and the object (*dhyeya*) of meditation.
Dhyeya	:	Object of meditation
Dvaidha	:	Division, separation into two parts

Dvaita-advaita : Duality-nonduality

Dvaitavādin : Those who assert two (*dvaita*) principles or existence of human soul as separate from the Supreme Being. In contrast, the Advaitavādin assert identity of Brahman or Paramātmana or Supreme Soul with Jīvātmā or human soul

GHI

Gṛihastha : Householder

Granthi : Psychic tangle or complex viz., Brahma, Vishṇu, Rudra Granthis

Guṇa : Attributes, qualities (Sattva, Rajas, Tamas)

Ichchā : Will, desire

Indriyas : Five Karmendriyas or powers of action and Five Buddhendriyas or Jñānendriyas or powers of sense-perception

J

Jagat : The Universe; the world process

Jīva : The individual soul which becomes identical with the Absolute (Śiva) after liberation

Jīvanamukta : To be liberated while still living and not "conditioned by limitation of his subtle and gross constitution"

Jīvātman : Individual soul

Jñāna : Spiritual wisdom

Jñānendriyas : Five powers of sense-perception i.e. smelling, tasting, seeing, touch, hearing

K

Kaivalya : Absolute unity; perfect detachment of soul from matter leading to emancipation

Kalās : Different kinds of Śaktis

Kāma : Longing

Kāya-sādhana : A way to achieve *deha-siddhi* regarded as necessary for realizing the Sahaja state

Kāya-siddhi : State which leads to Niryutthāna and realization pf Paramapada

Kshudra-brahmāṇḍa : Microcosm, the human body

Kuṇḍalinī Śakti	:	The Central Creative Power (of Śiva); spiritual power latent in every person; Divine Power conceived as existing in the form of a sleeping serpent closely embracing the lowest center of physical, vital and psychical energy, seed of all manifestation, Power of Śiva, infinite, dynamic, eternal during self-manifestation and immanent in the transcendent nature of Śiva
Kula	:	The state in which Śiva and Śakti remain in indistinguishable unity
Kula Śakti	:	Manifests herself in five forms — Parā, Sattā, Ahaṃtā, Sphurtā and Kalā, regarded as eternal and unfathomable
Kumbhaka	:	Retention of breath in the lungs

L

Lakshaṇa	:	Signs or attributes
Lakshya	:	Object of concentration inside the body or outside the body or without any reference to the body
Laya	:	Dissolution, interiorization of Consciousness
Loka	:	Plane of existence; a division of the universe, such as Bhūr-loka (the earth), Bhuvar-loka (the space between the earth *and the sun) and four others*

M

Maheśvara	:	Parama (the Highest) Śiva
Mana	:	Empirical mind
Manas	:	That aspect of mind which along with the senses builds perception, images and thought-constructs
Mano-vṛittis	:	Mental modifications
Matsara	:	Envious disposition, greed
Mātṛikā	:	The Parāvāk Śakti that generates the world
Māyā	:	Unreality; in Śāṁkara Vedānta, that which brings about illusion of the world
Mīmāṃsā	:	Profound thought or reflection, discussion

Moha	:	Delusion, attachment
Moksha	:	Liberation of Jivātmā from the cycle of birth and death. On attaining it one abides in the Divine Self.
Mudrā	:	Yogic control of certain organs to assist in concentration and in awakening Kuṇḍalinī for its journey to Sahasrāra. Also used for the Kuṇḍala which the Nāthas wear in their ears and which symbolize the light of Supreme Consciousness and bliss.
Mukti	:	Absorption in Brahman; liberation from bondage
N		
Nāda	:	Śelf-revelation of Śiva in sound form; transcendental sound heard as an inner sound when meditation reaches a certain stage. It is eternal and so regarded as Brahma-rūpa
Nāḍīs	:	Carriers of Prāṇa
Nijā-Śakti	:	Immanent in Para-Brahma Parameśvara; His pure Will, infinite, dynamic power inherent in the transcendent nature of Para Brahma (Śiva); self-manifestation of Śiva in the form of continuous evolution.
Nija-tattva-svarūpa	:	Ātmā or soul
Nirākāra	:	Formless
Nirguṇa	:	Having no epithet, attributes
Nirlipta	:	Unattached
Nirodha	:	To hold back or check, control; annihilation
Nirvāṇa	:	Dissolution in Śunya, liberation
Nirvikalpa	:	Devoid of all thought — constructs
Nirvikalpa-samādhi	:	In this there is final liberation and feeling of oneness with the Supreme Reality
Nirvyutthāna	:	Absorption in the Universal Consciousness, a stage higher than Samādhi and implies permanent illumined state in which one feels complete non-difference between the

		individual body and the Cosmic Body.
Nitya	:	Eternal
Niyama	:	Second *aṅga* of Yoga and includes internal i.e. mental and external purification, contentment, mortification, study, devotion to God and to dedicate all actions to Him.
O		
Oṁ	:	Manifesting word for Īśvara and all the various dieas about God; a most sacred word, the Supreme Light, the first *bīja* of the Vedas
P		
Pañcha-kula	:	Three guṇas (Sattva, Rajas, Tamas) along with Kāla and Jīva
Pañcha-Mahābhūtas	:	Five Physical elements which evolve from the Ādya Piṇḍa (Cosmic Body of Śiva)
Pañcharātra	:	Knowledge of the dissolution of the Universe and disappearance of the gross form of the Five Physical elements.
Para-Brahman	:	Supreme Spirit
Parā-Śakti	:	Highest Śakti immanent in Śiva. His *Ichchā* Śakti, *akhaṇḍa*, beyond name or form, inseparable from Him; the second stage of the self-unfoldment of the divine Śakti
Parā Vidyā	:	Which leads to the knowledge of Brahman
Parama	:	Highest
Parama Śiva	:	The Highest Reality
Paramānanda	:	Supreme bliss
Paramapada	:	Self luminous, undivided Universal Consciousness; Śiva with Chidrūpa-Śakti inhering in Him
Paramātmā	:	Supreme Soul or Spirit
Paramātma-bodha	:	Realization of the Supreme Soul
Parameśvara	:	Supreme Being, Supreme Reality
Parāpara	:	Intermediate stage, both identical and different; remote and proximate
Para-piṇḍa	:	Cosmic Body

Parā-Saṃvitta	:	Supreme Consciousness; the Absolute
Phala	:	Result of actions (of three types — visible (*dṛishṭa*), in the form of moral or religious merits or demerits (*adṛishta*) and *saṃskāra phala* which continue even in the next life due to their deep impression on mind
Piṇḍa	:	Body
Piṇḍa-Jñānī	:	Perfect knower of the body
Piṇḍa-saṃvitti	:	Understanding the Piṇḍa (body)
Piṇḍa-siddhi	:	A stage towards realizing the Paramapada
Pīṭha	:	Seat
Praṇava	:	Sacred word Oṁ
Prāṇāyāma	:	Controlling the motion of inhalation, exhalation and retention of prāṇa vāyu in the lungs; leads to the awakening of the Kuṇḍalinī Śakti by removing the coverings of *rajas* and *tamas* from the *chitta*.
Pralaya	:	Dissolution of the Universe
Prāṇa	:	Sum total of Cosmic Energy in each body, vital force, ever *chaitanya*; breath of life; generic name for vital power
Pratibha-jñāna	:	Knowledge which comes like a flash (about the nature of Jīva, Īśvara, Māya, etc.) Regarded as superior to the knowledge received from a guru.
Pratyāhāra	:	Withdrawal of senses from their objects (*vishaya*); restraining the external activity of the sense organs
Pūraka	:	Drawing in the air
R		
Rāga	:	Intense desire or attachment for an object; *rāga-dvesha* i.e. attachment and hatred
Rajas	:	A constituent of *prakṛiti* characterized by charity, desire for worldly enjoyments, wealth etc.
Rechaka	:	Throwing out the air or wind

S

Śabda-brahman	:	Ultimate Reality in the form of thought-vibration in which state thought and word are identical
Sachchidānanda	:	Consisting of existence, thought and joy
Sadguru	:	Self realized spiritual teacher
Sādhaka	:	An adept
Sahaja-jñāna	:	Knowledge of non-difference between Jīvātmā and Paramātmā.
Sahaja-Samādhi	:	Samādhi in normal waking state. Also called Jāgrata Samādhi
Sahasrāra	:	Highest lotus, the region of pure undimmed Consciousness, the realm of Śiva. Kuṇḍalinī on reaching there is believed to enjoy blissful experience of identity of the individual soul with the Supreme Spirit
Śakti	:	The power of Śiva to manifest, to maintain the manifestation and to withdraw it
Śakti-chakra-krama	:	Emergence of Nijā, Parā, Aparā, Sūkshmā or Vimarsha and Kuṇḍalinī Śaktis leading to the emergence of Para-Pinḍa, the Supreme Divinity
Śakti-pāta	:	Descent of Śakti; Divine grace by which the individual turns to and realizes his essential divine nature, some times it comes like a flesh
Sākāra	:	Having form, shape
Samadṛishṭi	:	Undifferentiated attitude
Samādhi	:	Stage of *dhyāna* or meditation when there is consciousness of only the object (*dhyeya*) and there is total absorption of the self-consciousness in the Supreme Consciousness and there is no duality between the person who is meditating and the object of meditation; also described as the state of non-difference between the Jīvātmā and Paramātmā
Samarasakaraṇa	:	Absorption in the Supreme

		Consciousness which continues even when not engaged in formal meditation
Sāmarasya	:	Identity, absorption in Universal Consciousness
Saṃkalpa	:	Conception or ideas or notion formed in the mind or heart
Saṃkucha	:	Contract
Saṃyama	:	Holding together; Dhāranā, Dhyāna, Samādhi practiced together in relation to the same object (dhyeya)
Śaucha	:	Internal and external purification, the former by cultivating the virtues of friendliness, mercy, cheerfulness, contentment and *tapa* or mortification.
Shaḍāṅga (yoga)	:	Six limbs or parts (of Yoga)
Shaṭ-chakra	:	The Six Centres (Mūlādhāra, Svadhishṭhāna, Maṇipūra, Anāhata, Viśuddha and Ājñā), the main stages of Śakti on her way to Sahasrāra
Siddha	:	One who has attained the highest object; endowed with super-natural faculties
Siddhis	:	Supernatural faculties, regarded as obstacles to the highest goal i.e. the attainment of the true knowledge of Self and realization of the Supreme Spirit
Śiva	:	Universal Consciousness, endowed with all the Śaktis and source of all phenomenal things
Śiva-svarūpa	:	Of the nature of Śiva
Śiva-Vyāpti	:	Realization of the world as an aspect of Self
Sopāya-jñāna	:	Consciousness of one's true nature or real Self (in essence the Supreme Soul)
Spaṅda	:	Primordial creative impulse
Sṛishṭi	:	Universe, manifestation
Sṛishṭi Kuṇḍalinī	:	One of the many name of Kuṇḍalinī as she creates the gross physical world
Sūkshma-śarīra	:	Inner subtle body
Śūnya	:	A state in which no object is experienced; four kinds of Śūnya associated with four stages in Yoga

Sva-prakāśa	:	Self-luminous
Svarūpa	:	Essential or real nature
Svarūpa-jñāna	:	Knowledge of Self
Svasaṃvedya	:	To be known or understood by oneself

T

Tamas	:	One of the constituents of Prakṛiti characterized by ignorance, anger, lust, pride, dullness etc.
Tanmātrā	:	The primary elements of perception *śabda, sparśa, rūpa, rasa, gandha.*
Tapa	:	Self mortification
Tattva-chintaka	:	Seeker of the Reality
Tattva-jñāna	:	Brahman-knowledge; knowledge of the Reality
Tattvas	:	Constitutive Principles and elements
Turīya	:	Fourth state of consciousness beyond the state of waking, dreaming and deep sleep; the state in which mind becomes free from the habits and *vāsanās* of previous lives, state of Chidānanda-consciousness and bliss
Turyātīta	:	State of Consciousness beyond the Turīya state in which Jīva is established in Nivikalpa samādhi

U

Uchchāra	:	Utterance
Unmanī	:	The stage of *dhyāna* in which there is no cessation of continuity in the identity of Self with the Supreme Spirit; highest state of consciousness when Māyā ceases completely; absorption (*laya*) of *chtita* in Nāda
Upaśam	:	To gain peace (by controlling the senses)
Upādāna (kāraṇa)	:	Proximate (cause)
Upadeśa	:	Teaching, instruction
Upāsya	:	Object of reverence or worship and *dhyāna* or meditation

V

Vairāgya	:	Indifference towards worldly objects; detachment from worldly pleasures
Vāk	:	Speech (its five *rūpa* or form or stages are

		Parā (urge for self-expression), *Paśyantī* — (Vāk at mental stage, not in any sound form), *Madhyamā* (stage between *Paśyantī* and articulate sound-speech), *Vaikharī* (audible spoken word), *Mātṛikā* (ultimate phonetic constituents of Vaikharī Vāk)
Vedya	:	That which is learnt
Viśrānti	:	Cessation; repose achieved by annihilation of *chitta-vṛittis*; state in which the Cosmic Body and the individual body are in undifferentiated state
Vikāras	:	Deviation, mental or physical, from the normal
Vikalpa	:	Thought-constructs
Virāṭa-Purusha	:	Cosmic Personality
Vishaya	:	The objects of the five *indriyas* or senses, each having its own *vishaya* or object viz., *śabda* or sound for the ear, *sparśa* or touch for the skin, *rūpa* (form or colour) for the eye, *rasa* (savour) for the tongue, *gandha* (odour) for the nose; worldly or sensual enjoyments
Vṛitti	:	Thought-constructs; nature, disposition
Vyāpti-vyāpaka-bhāva	:	Feeling of inseparableness and pervasiveness
Vyashṭi-piṇḍa	:	Individual body
Vyoma	:	Space, conceived in five different ways to facilitate concentration of mind
Vyoma-Pañchaka	:	The five Ākāśa (Ākāśa, Parākāśa, Mahākāśa, Tattvākāśa, Śūnyākāśa)

Y

Yoga	:	Science or knowledge which leads to the attainment of *moksha* and Tattva-jñāna; also defined as the union of Jīvātmā and Paramātmā; restraining the chitta-vṛittis so that the seer (Purusha) can see his own true nature

INDEX

¤ ¤ ¤

Seven Figures of the Chakras

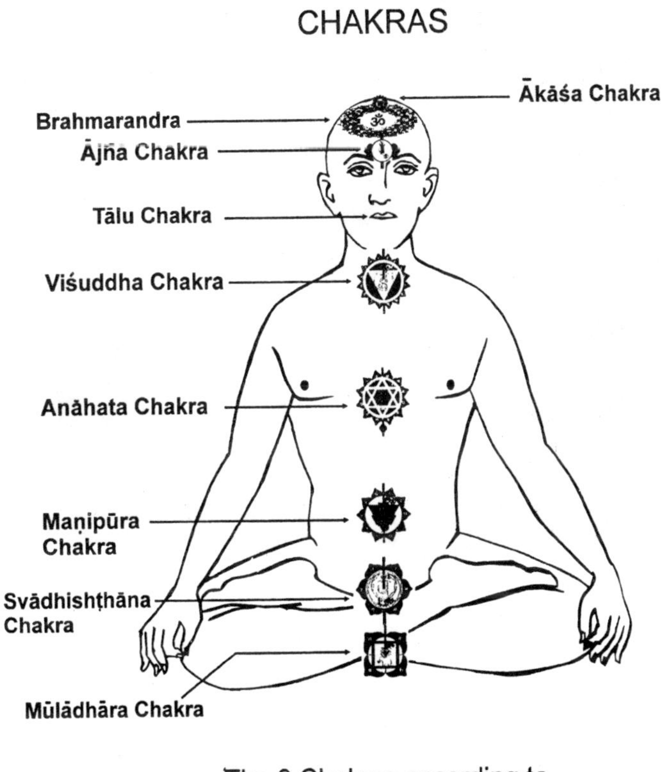

The 9 Chakras according to Gorakshanātha

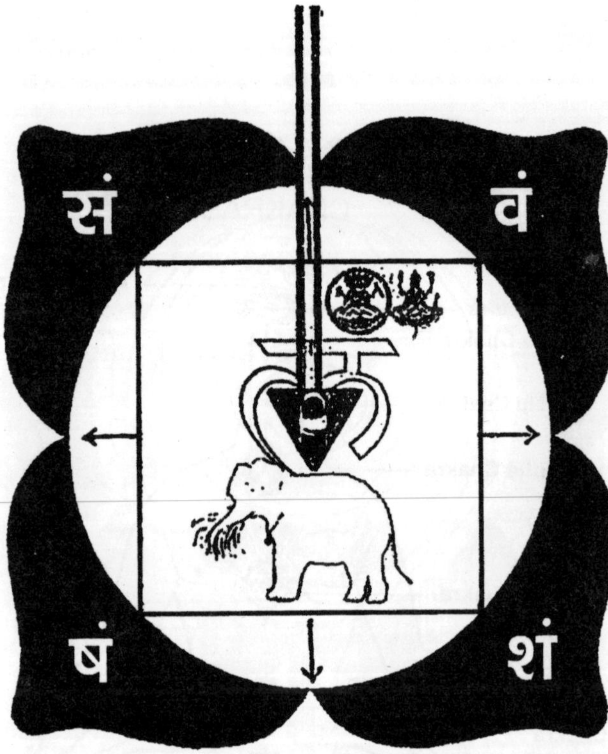

1. Mūlādhāra Chakra, **4 Petals**

Letters व, श, ष, स (Va, Śa, Sha, Sa)

with Bindu superimposed

2. Svādhishṭhāna Chakra, 6 Petals
Letters ब, भ, म, य, र, ल (Ba, Bha, Ma, Ya, Ra, La)
with Bindu superimposed

3. Maṇipūra Chakra, 10 Petals
Letters ड, ढ, ण, त, थ, द, ध, न, प, फ
(Ḍa, Ḍha, Ṇa, Ta, Tha, Da, Dha, Na, Pa, Pha)
with Bindu superimposed

4. Anāhata Lotus, 12 Petals
Letters क, ख, ग, घ, ङ, च, छ, ज, झ, ञ, ट, ठ
(Ka, Kha, Ga, Gha, Ṅa, Cha, Chha, Ja, Jha, Ña, Ṭa, Ṭha)
with *anusvāra* over them.

5. VIŚUDDHA, 16 Petals

Viśuddha-chakra with 16 petals
Letters: All the 16 Vowels beginning with A and ending with Visarga Aḥ (अः) with Bindu Superimposed

6. Ājñā Chakra, 2 Petals

Letters क्ष, ह (Ksha, Ha) with Bindu superimposed